Cover photo : *OPALKA 1965/1- ∞ Détail 1-35327*

Special thanks to:
Elisabeth Lagane, Stéphane Argillet, Stephen Wright

this series edited by
JACINTO LAGEIRA

in the same series

JEAN-MARC BUSTAMANTE
Christine Macel, Marc Perelman, Jacinto Lageira

DAN GRAHAM
Alain Charre, Marie-Paule Macdonald, Marc Perelman

GERHARD RICHTER
Gertrud Koch, Luc Lang, Jean-Philippe Antoine

3, RUE BEAUTREILLIS
75004 PARIS
ISBN 2-906571-57-1

PRINTED IN FRANCE

Roman Opalka

CHRISTINE SAVINEL
JACQUES ROUBAUD
BERNARD NOËL

CONTENTS

Opalka or the Ethics of Assignation

When he chose in 1965 to dedicate the rest of his life, as an artist and as a man, to the realization of this one project, complex but unique; to paint, write, tell and photograph every day, recording the act of living and every instant of the act of painting, Roman Opalka gave himself an assignment for life. This artistic project, which is also his major work, is driven by great ambition: it pursues unicity, it implies the radicalization of an artistic system which in turn programs his entire life. For this project which also shows an enigmatic side, Opalka claims an ethical quality. The assigment is meant to be total, involving the whole subject, all subjects: the artist's ego, the painter himself, compelled because of a choice supposedly free at the origin, to pursue the program thus imposed exclusively and rigorously; and the subject represented, committed as well, by reflection. They are inseparable since the painter will never more cease to trace, draw, paint the series of increasing numbers starting from the digit 1, placed, with emotion, right at the top on the left hand side of the first canvas in 1965. They are inseparable since this counting corresponds to the flow of Opalka's life itself, and since the painter has chosen his own vital mortal countdown, as subject. His project entitled OPALKA 1965/1 - ∞ is thus unique by definition. And this total embodiment is also the true originality of an artistic process, which nevertheless is within the mainstream of characteristic works after World War II and particularly in the sixties, by its attempt to propose an artistic solution, viable still, and which would be its own origin in a sense. This is true of most esthetic movements of that period, but, closer to Opalka (if there is any sense in such a statement) we may think of Barnett Newman for example, Agnes Martin, and especially Ad Reinhardt, perhaps the most comparable, since he too assigned for himself, from 1957 until his death, the realization of a single painting, of the same size and always black. But there is one main difference among others, which Opalka notes so rightly: the staging and the *mise en œuvre*, in a kind of intimate yet complex performance, of the artist Opalka painting the number and the texture of the time granted to him, while implementing to the letter (that of the number) in the transcription he makes of it, its own inexorable specificity.

For this deliberate assignment, the involvement of his vital time, Roman Opalka thus sets an ethical quality. The word often appears in the very long monologue that constitues the main part of the fine work consecrated (the proper term) to him at the behest of Pierre Brochet, at La Hune press[1]. The frequency of this qualification attracts attention, just as the need to comment endlessly on his work and indicate the protocol for a good reading. This exegetic verbosity contrasts paradoxically with the characteristic reserve of the artistic process. But in fact one can see the problems linked to such an undertaking, so clearly solipsist, elaborated over the years with obsessional care: the representation of the counting absorbs the life of the painter, who paints the numbers white on a background prepared in black, then in gray, *Detail* after *Detail* (each painting bears this same title, followed by the first then the last number depicted); until 1992, whenever he travelled, he would interrupt his painting only to draw his *Cartes de voyage*, with ink on paper. The artistic system also includes the photographic self-portraits, taken at the end of every day's work; and finally the voice, for since he undertook, in 1972, on reaching the figure of a million, to add systematically to the black background one percent of white to each new canvas, Opalka decided to tape his voice in Polish counting out part of the series of numbers, in anticipation of the moment when he would be, perhaps, painting white on white ("the imprints of the numbers are already difficult to make out" says he as early as 1987). His voice, his face, his time. But this claimed ethical nature does not only imply the evident rigorous quality of his personal assignment, but a value of alterity, as well, which is still to be shown. Just as is the legitimity of the reference to infinity, to the divine at times, which suggests that ethics are here understood as a means to enable one to surpass oneself and attain the sublime. The reality of the personal involvement would refer to a truth—a term also used by the artist. In the same way the matter of Opalka's position in the contemporary art world is considered, and one can see straightaway that this superb isolation must be subject to a more arduous justification. Finally the main reason that makes one want to think about his œuvre, its extreme beauty, the fascination of these waves of signs that come to life, from a distance, in big swells, the seduction of the grays, the joy in the extreme attention one must have, closely this time, to the minute variations in the configuration, in the

[1] Roman Opalka, *OPALKA 1965/1-∞*, Paris, La Hune, 1992.

shades, the syntax of the canvas, all these matters, as well as the emotion that amazingly takes hold of the spectator, somewhat bely the intended rigor (would beauty thus be the only tolerable incident?), and lead us to challenge this ethical claim again, refusing to believe the artist straightaway or take his word for it, apart from the vital, mortal implication, which is undeniably his. But first of all, for rigor, there is the one imposed upon him, and then chosen, or re-chosen, going from penury to sobriety.

Deprivation

> "Good-evening. Mine is a faint voice. Kindly tune accordingly. (Pause) Good-evening. Mine is a faint voice. Kindly tune accordingly. (Pause) It will not be raised, nor lowered, whatever happens. (Pause) Look. (Long pause) The familiar chamber. (Pause) At the far end a window. (Pause) On the right the indispensable door. (Pause) On the left, again the wall, some kind of pallet. (Pause) The light: faint, omnipresent. No visible source. As if all luminous. Faintly luminous. No shadow. (Pause) No shadow. colour; none. All gray. Shades of gray. (Pause) The colour gray if you wish, shades of the colour gray. (Pause) Forgive my stating the obvious."[2]

Beckett, to whom Opalka refers at times, mostly to qualify the essence of his *wait*, by analogy with characters who are waiting for Godot, shows an amazingly similar material universe. And this opening scene of the television play *Ghost Trio*, is an exemplary display of deprivation, and its obvious strength is the obviousness of the rule. All that can constitute deprivation is in it, necessarily. All that characterizes the life of Roman Opalka and his work. As discreet as he may be on the subject, he must admit having known all kinds of deprivation in his childhood, from the extreme poverty of his family to the deportation to Germany at the age of nine. Solitude, fear, incarceration, Opalka can not or wishes not to be more loquacious about these depths of distress, speaking of one deprivation just to avoid mentioning the other. He has them almost codified in two stories (we wish to avoid the term anecdotes) that are repeated from one interview to the next (each time you think he will not say the same thing, but he does). About the camps, there is one memory of his solitude in jail, where he made a little ball to play with, out of ersatz wool from a blanket—from which he draws a moral of survival, of adjustment. When asked to say more, he prefers to go back to the poverty of his childhood, to assert that the worst memory lies there, in his terror, as a poor child who, staying at home, alone, was supposed to touch nothing, would merely watch the clock pendulum; which stopped one day, due to his glance, he thought at

[2] Samuel Beckett, *Ghost Trio,* in *ends and odds*, Grove Press, New York, 1976.

the time. The absolute terror of having broken the most precious belonging of the family, the terror, he says nowadays, of having stopped the flow of the world. Here, modesty bonders on the elaboration of the personal myth, and these two stories are as basic as they are reserved. Opalka's life continues for a while in poverty. In postwar Poland, he lives for a time, sharing a room of nine square meters, where he sleeps — here is Beckett's hovel — on a couch so dilapidated that he falls through several times a night. This state of things ends with the start of his career as an artist, a few prizes from foreign countries, a few commissioned works, of course.

Opalka goes back to all of this, transforming endured hardships into an esthetically chosen experience. There are a few exceptions, a few redresses, the most spectacular of which is the raising of the man-artist, who will always wish to paint standing, in front of his canvas and therefore did not follow Pollock in his new positionings versus the canvas. (One may note Opalka's need of an unquestionable symbolism, for there are other noble postures, for example, Ad Reinhardt, sitting and bending over his canvas with the modesty of an artisan). But on the whole, Roman Opalka's esthetic and plastic process will undergo a succession of deprivations, determined, self-inflicted, and then chosen.

Already his paintings from before his big project, his *Chronomes*, for example, did not allow much: little variety, no representation, small abstract figures, in tight lines, announcing the flow of numbers. But, the *Details* impose an absolute renouncement of variety, of differences; and only variations remain, all of which are planned. Yet Opalka impugns what could be an accusation of monotony, considering his painting as an action "where repetition is just an appearance." Stating himself as an "active-anti-Sisyphus," he reintroduces the primordial idea of the representation and of the inscription of time in his work, while underlining its performance aspect. Nevertheless there remains the refusal of all variety foreign to the project, and to the normal effect of surprise, which becomes, paradoxically, the surprise of monotony.

And then, in the *Chronomes* there was still some color. Red is Opalka's temptation. It's still true at the beginning of the program and there are two *Details* very much appreciated by collectors for their rare red background. The renouncement of color is described with exceptional dramatic force. When he was in West Germany, his lady friend Halszka Pierkarczyk, in agreement with Wladyslava Jaworska, a distinguished art critic who always defended his work, asked him to bring back, for her, the biggest possible amount of tubes of color. Thus does Opalka relate the anecdote:

"With great care, I fulfiled this order. I even applied myself to choose, for her, countless shades, with the state of mind of a painter who wishes to use all the power of color very freely. Back in Warsaw, I presented her with the tubes. Right away my lady friend tells me she has been speaking with Wladyslawa and that they had come to the conclusion that it was impossible for me to devote myself exclusively to the realization of all my *Details*."

The aim is here to show the resistance his project encountered, but it is impossible not to hear, in the insistance with which he describes his own careful attention and the feeling of power and of freedom before the infinity of the tones, a sort of solemn mourning for color. Opalka will mention this deprivation no more, and when he adds photography to his program, he chooses black and white, of course (one is tempted to say gray and white). A political dimension is added to his renouncement of the color red, linked, says he, to his rejection of communism. With slightly moral irony, the color red was given back to him by his current lady friend, Marie Madeleine, whose color it is. The joy detectible when he relates that (to Pierre Brochet and Christian Schlatter in Delphi) is indeed a private matter, but symbolic also. The choice of gray, with Opalka, rather resembles an obligation. A self-inflicted obligation, of course. But rarely do the violence and the constraint of the assignation he imposed on himself appear as clearly. Moderate most of the time and reserved in his statements, he feels the urge to express himself in a strong way, speaking of "pictoral sacrifice," and even slipping towards an expressionist lyricism, when he qualifies gray as a "deadly emotional" color. Such a power of deprivation of color is purely that of the painter, thanks to which he recreates the whole palette within gray, all the shades, as if transposed in an atonal modality, in each canvas, in all of his work in progress, in his photographs too. An appealing palette of gray shades (Beckett: "the colour gray, if you wish") a ghostly palette of colors he deprived himself of (Beckett: "colour: none").

With the addition of photography, he reverts apparently on the deprival of figurative representation, human among others. But the matter requires more nuances. On one hand there has always been "body" in the project: from the measurement of the artist's hand, chosen as spacing between each canvas in the exhibitions, to the size of the canvas determined by his own height (as with Ad Reinhardt, for the size of his ultimate painting), Opalka's body is present all over; by the skin too, because the idea of tattooing comes to mind inevitably; and more abstractly, there is a sort of accountancy of the body of the painting, in its process but also in its texture. On the other hand, in photography, the total identical similarity of the subject right to the desired expression, if it does not dehumanize in the least, confers a certain quality of abstraction. Finally, apart from the strictly objective representation, it is difficult to measure here what the artist deprives himself of, or not, as to the body—one can say for example that in his accounting-painting, there is only his body in action, and that, in a sense, in the photographs, it is missing. Deprivation here, goes beyond the specific esthetic program, to meet the condition of absence which marks the image in general.

All things considered, Opalka wished to deprive himself of novelty (to protect himself against it?). That is to say, of the temporal form of alterity. Never more another color apart from gray, another sign apart from the number, another face apart from mine. Never more another size, another paint brush (his program includes the tools of its realization, the paint brush is always the same, a Rowney number 0). Never more another project. Because there will never be another time than the one allowed to me. The justification is unanswerable, being mortal condition. Opalka thus deprives himself of the reversibility of time, beneath the different formes that this delusion may take, starting with memory. In his project, the purpose will not be the evocation of a long-lost time, but to leave a trace of this instant of life-in-art.

By depriving himself of the possibility of novelty, Opalka, a painter of the second half of the twentieth century, left the art movement, or more precisely set himself up in an unreachable enclave, somewhere along the line of the evolution of art theories and forms. His unconditional refusal of what he calls "the vanity of novelty" is not my subject here, apart from the fact that there is obviously an ethical dimension in such an esthetic and historical choice. Except for Yves Klein, and Ad Reinhardt, as well as Buren, Ryman and Pollock, Opalka often differs from his contemporaries—especially from American art. Of a strictly esthetic choice there would not be much to say, but through his ethical claim, he authorizes and encourages questioning about the legitimacy of this deprivation, which according to the evidence is a rejection. All of these deliberate refusals have corresponding advantages—the refusal of the useful opens the way to the poetical, the refusal of the representation allows a certain mystery, and the refusal of the possibility of novelty brings a kind of durable serenity into autonomy and timelessness, that may appear as desirable as dangerous. Right from the start, the rigor with which Opalka reproduces and incorporates in his œuvre the conditions of want that he had to suffer is admirable (instead of practicing for example a liberating expressionism or an easily compensating esthetic of excess), but one can clearly see how the application of this same principle to the history of art may have some perverse effects. If one refrains, at first, from considering the biographical reasons that may encourage Opalka, here again, to part from history in general, even the history of art, so that nothing new may ever appear that may harm the erection of his monument, one may be ill at ease when reading what he says about his program: "Although it is precisely the formal evolution of art that allowed it to take on this precise appearance, it could have been contemporary with the ideas of Pythagoras and Plato"; and moreover: "It's by abstracting myself from the formal problems of painting that I place my concept on the chessboard." Here we may say, that what was until now the rigor of claimed deprivation tends to become the latitude of ordained subtraction. The question is indeed to subtract oneself from a set of formal thoughts and practices, to which we owe our being, what we are; although wishing to keep our place in the milieu where they develop, but apart, on the side or facing (confronting, as in a game of chess, says Opalka), beyond perhaps. If the project remains unquestionable, this word takes on a different meaning: one must respect the proposition of the artist, admit that his freedom was at that price, that if he does not return to the art world whatever he got from it, insofar as he does not give steps by which other artists could continue in his path, in spite of obstacles, he offers the example of his sacrifice, temporal and non temporal, and the autonomy and the disinterestedness of his œuvre makes it a necessary testimony. If this attitude is still, for me, questionable, I find it nevertheless justifiable as it questions the capacity of the avant-garde and the logic of novelty. Dangerous only when it hopes to be beyond suspicion. But, with Opalka, the man is always so indissociable from the artist that this new form of intransigence is still understandable, so difficult is the absence of detachment, perhaps impossible. To suspect his project is to question the whole of his œuvre, of his life. Perhaps the artist must have an answer for each question when he answers for everything. That is, for one thing, himself.

"My responding singularity" (Emmanuel Lévinas) [3]

This adamantine rigor of what the artist refuses, and refuses to himself, this radical resolution, nearly *a priori*, of all the problems linked to the conception and materialization of an œuvre, everything converges and tends to unicity. There is, says Opalka, "but one painting," "but one concept," just as there is only one gesture to paint it, a single movement, one life: "the raison d'être of my program relies on an extreme determination to realize one and only one thing during the rest of my lifetime." The reason for his dissociation from other artists using the true numbers of their lives as material, but extracting a discontinuous, anecdotic œuvre from it, is specially clear here — On Kawara

[3] Emmanuel Lévinas, *Autrement qu'être, ou au-delà de l'essence*, Paris, Le Livre de Poche, 1974.

for example, sending his postcards and telegrams, erratically to mention what he is doing, or that he is still alive. With Opalka, the unicity of the process is everywhere: in the apparent monotony already mentioned, in the series of numbers straightaway evocative of all the sequence, etc. The radicality is impressive, the closure and the terminology are frightening at times, when the painter declares: "I have planned an œuvre that plans my life." We do not fear to see Opalka yielding to a totalitarian vision which he evidently suffered from—and besides he points out that this planification is his means to escape the system of production and consumption, for he paints slowly and produces few paintings—but we fear to find him the prisoner of such programming. It's quite the opposite, says he, and this rigorous unicity is his true freedom. The painting is unique and is its own justification, "The work bears its own proof," and "tests its own relevance." Such a logic is as unanswerable as it is indemonstrable. There is a rhetoric, even a poetic sense of oneness in Opalka, which declines all the possibilities of self-induced necessity, in, at times, an incantatory mode. We as observers must accept the postulate of a double existential justification of the œuvre. In the process (of being painted, counted), it is its own demonstration. It proves its feasability and its legitimacy all at once. It is what is (still) possible, it is what should be (must be) done. For the artist, the rewards of such a unitarian operation are immense, for they allow him to combine in an eternal moment the statement, the conception, execution of each *Detail*, of every *Detail*. It allows him to take a place in the history of art, a legitimate one, at a non-chronological point if one could say so.

The spectator has not much to say, since everything is done, thought and justified by the artist. Opalka—who does not exclude a religious dimension, non specific—puts the spectator in the position of contemplating an icon. Beyond the esthetic pleasure, he relieves the spectator of any need to judge, asking him to believe what he sees, to believe without proof of course, on his word, or on his number. Less constraining and less icon-like, are, in reality, the paintings of Newman, Martin or Reinhardt, which remain open to the indefinite world of meditation without object. (Hence the frequent desire of the art critics to determine this object —as in the exhibition, *Negotiating Rapture* which is now at the Museum of Contemporary Art of Chicago) [4]. With Opalka, on the contrary, the object is present, unforgettable. Even to the spectator unaware of the project, these regular lines of numbers in sequence speak of time; if he looks at the canvas without reading it, as a whole, the emphasis of the white due to each new application of paint, with the darker

[4] *Negotiating Rapture*, Chicago, Museum of Contemporary Art, 1996.

intervals, creates a scansion suggesting time once again. Then, once he examines it more closely, looks at the photographs along with a few *Details* and thinks of the voice that is counting, or hears it, the spectator is indeed caught up in a different time, constraining and literally fascinating: the time of this man's life. Unlike his usual reaction to contemporary art work, the spectator is here asked to contemplate an icon of the time of a man's life, or of an artist's mortality. One may suppose that the ideal way of looking at Opalka's work would be to reach a peak of contemplation or empathy such that the time of looking is nullified and blended with that of the work. This forced passivity leaves us facing another radical alternative: feeling useless, far outside the project, or on the contrary implicated literally and entirely. The postulated reaction of the spectator is thus specific, and rather than postulated, it is induced by the project, made necessary (not for the program, for us). In front of the esthetic and philosophical propositions of a Duchamp, or a Warhol, it is a matter of reaction; and curiously, the same goes for a Reinhardt or a Ryman, in a different way, but the spectator does answer in return. As for one of Opalka's *Details*, on the contrary, it is no longer a matter of answering to but of answering for. All things considered, the spectator ends up feeling having been himself already present or included in the number 1 of the first *Detail*, just as in the "Mon unicité de répondant". He is then really Opalkian, if such a thing is possible.

This matter of the reception of an œuvre has to do with the matter of alterity, and thus with the possibility of true ethics, of a position where personal rigor eludes solipsism. Yet Opalka insists constantly on the fact that there is only himself in his œuvre. He himself put together all the elements of the case often made against him. There is only himself, and his œuvre is his own "embodiment." The very long monologue in the La Hune book is not only a text in the first person, which is the rule of the genre, but a text about the first person—my concept, my project, my existence, my death. And nevertheless in this text is understood and in this project is clearly shown a concept and a syntax that could correspond to the beautiful phrase of Emmanuel Lévinas, an "intrigue de responsabilité." It appears in the structure of the reception such as I have put forwards, where the oneness of the œuvre incites paradoxically the division of its legitimacy and of its responsibility. But in a no less paradoxical way, it is at the heart of the very conception of the subject, as exposed as he may be. For instance when he says "my procedure manifests nothing apart from the duration of a lifetime," Opalka clearly puts his purpose at the service of the representation of (a) life, the article having an indefinite value, not a selective one. In what he calls his sacrifice, the artist purposes to testify to the life of any man through his. He is, in a sense, still according to Lévinas's terms, "required...by the responsibility" (the entire quotation is "requis, en-deçà de l'essence, par la responsabilité"). The responsibility of exposing oneself, of using oneself, to testify.

One must also look at the way he does expose himself, and in what measure he himself is the subject or an exemplary *He*. The observation of the lithographs or engravings he produced between 1967 and 1970 is quite enlightening in that respect. A photolithography of 1967, *C'est la lutte finale*, created indeed for the fiftieth anniversary of the October Revolution, represents, in red monochrome, a dense crowd that fills all the space, in which one sees, apart from the first row, only faces crushed against one another; in the foreground, one finds again, in the mirror, the same faces, more blurred. In *De Kronstadt à Vladivostok/Les marins de la mer noire* (1967), the color is blue, the crowd of sailors well-ordered in even lines of faces, in series nearly rectilinear, like the strokes of the sabres. Beyond the commissioned work, how can we help seeing the series of faces foreshadowing the series of numbers, the time of the life and of the painting of Opalka becoming painted numbers covering and representing the faces of the crowd of the oppressed—victims in one way or another. An engraving of 1968, *La Terre,* from a fragment of Eisenstein's picture representing the attack of the Winter Palace in Saint-Petersburg in 1917, shows once again a crowd in tight rows, more stylized, and is particularly close to the effect produced by the design and the rhythm of the *Cartes de voyage*. The enumeration of the life of the artist includes the other as well, all the others, the crowd of all the others, taken here moreover in a great historical movement of which they are at the at once the object and the subject. As for the last etching ever realized by Opalka (for which he got the prize of the 7th biennial of engravings in Tokyo in 1970), it again represents a crowd of faces crushed against one another, with moreover an admirable effect of nearness and remoteness: on the top and on the bottom, two waves of faces near enough to be identified as such; and as if springing from these waves, the swell of faces drawn back on the sides, to meet in the middle of the engraving, in the farthest background, forming but a mist of points. The title is: *And I will make your descendants as the dust of the earth, so that if a man can count the dust of the earth then shall your descendants also be counted.* (Gen: 13). The chain is all ready, for if one cannot count the dust of the earth, one may count the dust of one's own moments, as they pass by, and through them, testify to all the descendants of the world. In this splendid engraving, the connection between the white and the black, the effect of the gray, the scansion effect, everything is close to the *Details*, down to the counting, which precisely will be the means to count the countless numbers of the other, here represented.

The counting itself is as a graphic, plastic, "plotting of responsibility."

If we should turn our attention to the photographic self-portraits of Opalka, still with the concern of determining the position of the subject towards the other in his vision, we see at first that everything is planned with obsessional care and precision. The conditions for realization are required and the dispositions form a rule. Is it hence a matter of an obsession with oneself? Opalka relates how he put together the ritual over the years, more exactly how the choices imposed themselves, in accordance with the truth of the project. Thus the need to wear the same white shirt. Or to show, as much as possible, the same expression every day. Which is in my opinion, to the contrary of what may appear, furthest from narcissism—precisely all the further since it seems near. Already in the very conception, without images, the idea of aiming at a uniformity of expression, each day (and despite what may have happened during the day, even the death of the father, says he in a discreet way) tends to a neutralization of his own emotions. Happiness, pains, tempers, incidences of what might have happened on that day, all is erased deliberately as expression—where one sees Opalka apply to his own image and his own face his violently anti-expressionist credo. Thus remains the imprint of the effect of these emotions on his face, their inscription, counted and measured in furrowing wrinkles, tired glances, pallor of the lips. Without forgetting the effects of this erasure of expression, which is perhaps the most stirring. Obvious, then, the white shirt, to maintain the general whitening, of the hair, of the skin, of the photograph as it seems. Opalka adds that after having tried a new camera, which made pictures that were too clear, he returned to the old one, which will grow old with him. One might see a tendency to fetishism or esthetism. But, here I see another proof of that detachment which involves self-investment: the sharp photographical representation would accentuate the detail of his image, the relative blurness contributes to a relative neutralization, which allows exemplarity (of aging, of tiredness, of pain). With the photographs at the end of the chain, the counting is back to human, and the face of Roman Opalka can represent that of the innumerable other, and answer to his sufferings.

One must also look at other photographs, that are not elements which compose the œuvre, but apart from it, as documents bearing on the program. Yet such a separation is questionable in a sense: if one admits that the realization of this œuvre includes a performance, the latter calls for and includes all the photos (moreover the ones I am looking at in the La Hune book were chosen with the artist's approuval). So for instance, photographed in his studio, from the back, in his white suit, a perfectly straight little silhouette in the beam of the spotlights, surrounded by microphones, encircled by photographs, painting, visibly but not ostentatiously holding the paintbrush in one hand, the jar of paint in the other. Opalka manages to be singular and exemplary, moving in his singularness and his exemplariness. There is no one but him, and he so little of him. The same photograph of this place where he paints, taken without him, and meant to demonstrate the non-interruption of his œuvre during his absence, makes us realize not merely how, when he is not there, he is there nevertheless, but also that when he is there, he is hardly there. And then is a wonderful little photograph in black and white, gray tints with in the mirror, bearing the title *Accrochage*, shows the artist highly attentive as he seems to be towards himself, from the back, white hair in the foreground, white shirt, hanging up one of his photographic self-portraits with a minimun of movement. And precisely, it is in the quality of the attention that he has for himself, that he has for this image of himself that is his œuvre, in the precision of the visible gesture, as in the exactness of the gaze suggested by the angle of the face raised slightly towards the photograph, that one may grasp the realm beyond oneself, though he is quite alone. All of his gestures are "required," all the images of him, a primary or secondary ones. "Required, by the responsability" to show every thing, to show the one in oneself.

Such would be thus the specific form of Opalkian ethics, that self-detachment from oneself. But one must still admit that singularity is never eliminated, and it is at the heart of the program that the matter is at the same time, always, precisely, by name, Roman Opalka—OPALKA. And that the matter could never have not been him. Such are probably the limit and the stumbling-block of the reference to the thought of Emmanuel Lévinas, for there is not in Opalka that "selflessness" of self where the subject occurs, at the remotest from the self, thus at the nearest; but rather the possibility of letting the dust of the world (all the others and oneself) not so much occur as survive—while remaining nearest to oneself, counting the numbered days of human life, and watching for the death to come.

An exhausting accountancy

OPALKA 1965/1 - ∞ is a literally exhausting œuvre. As in the analysis done by Deleuze of Beckett's play, *Quad*[5], the exhaustiveness and the exhaustion are here linked, but the implication is different and the form specific. In *Quad*, all the possible figures are successively exhausted, with and by an appalling exhaustiveness. In OPALKA, it is different, for exhaustiveness and exhaustion each take a double form. A static form first of all, in reply to the vaguely mystic

[5] Gilles Deleuze, "L'Épuisé", in Samuel Beckett, *Quad & Le Trio du Fantôme*, Paris, Minuit, 1992.

vision of the 1. The unicity already mentioned is particularly interesting in its temporal aspect. Everything fully exists at each moment of the œuvre, since everything starts and all is accomplished at each instant. "In my concept," says Opalka, "the always finished part of my œuvre dates from 1965: the sign 1, laid on the first *Detail*, there is already all." And also: "A *Detail* is constantly definite," or else "with the non definite, I define the definite." It is the One of Parmenides, says he, and effectively we have but to re-read the *Parmenides* of Plato: "Then the existent one is apparently, both one and many, a whole and parts limited and of infinite number"; or else the fragment of the *Parmenides* of Elea: "so that it is not right for what-is to be incomplete. For it is not lacking; what-is-not would lack everything" [6]. The idea is here analogous, as is similar this essentially paradoxal configuration that defines the definite (in the sense of completeness) by the impossibility of the in-de-finite. The opposite and complementary demonstration, being of the structure of the *Dasein* (while operating on other particulars) may also be part of the Opalkian program: it is because definite is (in the sense of an obviously individualized perception) that there is infinite.

Thus the One and the 1. Not the zero of Suprematism as with Malevitch, not the zero of Duchamp, seen by Opalka as a search for the degree 0 of the sensitivity of the artist. The one of the origin, which is at the origin of his own system. Which is also its finality. In fact, if you look at a *Detail* now, any one, you see the totality of the numbers in it, from 0 to 9, in combinations and sequences that vary usually very slightly, but at times radically (for the passing of the tens, the hundreds, etc.). And then, but it is more difficult to see when you look at a *Detail* for the first time, the (supposedly) flawless sequence implies the continuity of the design, and even its exhaustiveness, whether the rest of the design is material or not. The numbering attests to a whole, the scansion overflows the canvas.

But with this second aspect of the plastic representation of the one, a dynamic is engaged. For one must be clear about the nature of the One. Once again the "One" of Opalka, while exceeding the specific, remains at the same time the 1 of the first day of the œuvre, and the number one of his life. He establishes a second axis of exhaustion and exhaustiveness, dynamic and chronological this time. There lies his invention, which differentiates him from the Oneness of Streminski—whose influence he admits in the *Chronomes* (the analogy is evident, abstraction, monochromy, repetition of the same unique

[6] Plato, *Parmenides*, trad. H. N. Fowler, Harvard University Press, The Lœb Classical Library, 1939; *Parmenides of Elea on nature*, trad. Scott Austin, Yale University Press, 1986.

little motif). And what happens in the *Chronomes* is essential, for the comprehension of OPALKA 1965/1 - ∞. It is not that he grew weary of painting his *Chronomes*, it is that people read them wrongly, contenting themselves with formal considerations. His will to make the spectator read better is one of the direct causes of this setting in space and in signs. The sequential organisation will allow a scansion of the real time bestowed to the artist. The chronological accomplishment of an exhaustive program will be fulfilled with vital exhaustion precisely until death may come. The counting sequence is deadly. Of his accounted days the artist makes an œuvre.

The temporal system thus functions in a kind of *double-bind*, on the one hand in the exhaustion, each canvas (or *Carte de voyage*, or photograph) showing the precise, material exhaustion, of so much paint used, of so much time necessary, of that photo, of this ink, and even of that paintbrush (preciseness emphasized by the decision to use a new brush for each canvas, out of concern for the regularity with which the paint is applied); and in the exhaustiveness on the other hand, since this same *Detail* demonstrates, shows, defectively, by means of reference and logical necessity, the existence of all, of which it is the exhaustive representative. Exhaustiveness and exhaustion intersect along this *double-bind* to meet at last at the deadly horizon of this project—in fact they had never ceased working together. For all coheres in this, to say that Roman Opalka exhausts himself painting. He says: "I accept the progess of the physical pain imposed upon me by this work." And it is not an image. He relates that at the beginning of the project, the mere idea of this rule in which he was entering made him sick for several months. He lets us foresee that this painter's unique posture he has chosen and imposed on himself, constantly standing, his arms raised to the canvas, is not accomodating to the ageing body. Life runs dry to the increasing number, and to put this evident truth plastically into action is a harrowing ordeal. Opalka's text on passing the million mark says so:

> "At the beginning of a long period of time marked only by nine hundred thousand numbers, first series towards six times the number 9, as when walking in the desert, the approach of a coming oasis, that gives us the strength to carry on, with the prospect of the presence of the 9 for still ninety thousand numbers to reach the third element of the suite of 9, sensitive to the fact of having just nine thousand numbers to paint, after such a long route, and the nine hundred numbers nearer and nearer, the heart beating, the voice already quivering, then the ninety numbers, the breath winded as a runner in a sprint towards a stage, the hand shaking, marking only ninety numbers and thus so near six times the number 9 and reaching after nine numbers to paint calling them out in Polish, the voice choking with emotion, six different suites ascending and descending towards what separates me still from the same six

signs: dziewiecset dziewiecdzesiat dziewiec tysiecy dziewiecset dziewiecdziesiat dziewiec...: nine hundred ninety-nine thousand nine hundred ninety-nine which composes a sequence capable of expressing phonetically and chronologically always different meanings of the six numbers 9 so as to release from this number a horizontal space, another rhythm in the pursuuit of the same dynamics.[7]"

Opalka's literary temptation here produces a beautiful text, like a legend of numbers, a cruel story, an account of a station along the road of a chosen passion. To tell the emotion of the passing of the million, a single sentence, a single breath, scanned in several times ten periods articulated in a single suite. So there may be a suite. And since the risk of not crossing this ford is materialized with violence in the body: the heart beating, the shaking hand, the choking voice. Exhausted with emotion, the voice is about to choke. If Opalka added to his performance the taping of counting aloud, it is not only not to be lost on that far hypothetical day of the passing to white on white, but also, henceforth, for the reassuring deictic relay of the voice, the certainty that this counting, this passing the million for example, will have occurred—and that it was he who counted, painted, passed. Having experienced how easily the painter's voice could be muffled, even overshadowed, he decides now to materialize it physically, technically, by taping it. Sheer waste of course, but rescuing it also: "man is this being who does away with himself and, at the same time preserves himself—as unspeakable—in language[8]", (Giorgio Agemben). It is in this respect of harrowing relevance that Opalka has linked the necessity of taping his voice to his decision to go towards the "mental" white, associating suppression and conservation. In the Opalkian system, the voice is trace and index, it is what makes it impossible not to hear Roman Opalka indicate that he is really crossing the ford, from number to number.

Considering this text, and even though the painter tells us that each *Detail* is equally interesting, the painting that depicts passing the million mark, *Detail* 993460-1017875, is particularly moving, with its ultimate line of six particularly regular 9, where the painter catches his breath, the white on the brush fails slightly; so he takes more paint, gets his breath back, and traces the stroke of the1, very white, slightly separated (so that it's also the inital 1 that is recalled). When looking at the totality, passing from the slightly cramped, stooped, anxious lines of the 9 to series more widely spaced and stronger on the other side of the rediscovered 1, gives precisely the impression of gaining

[7] *OPALKA 1965/1-∞*, op. cit.; the first version of this text is in Roman Opalka, *OPALKA 1965/1-∞, Rencontre par la séparation*, XIXe Biennale internationale de São Paulo et Centre culturel de Buenos Aires, 1987.

[8] Giorgio Agemben, *Il linguagio e la morte*, Julio Einaudi Editore, 1982.

one's breath back. This 9 opening on to the 1, this dehiscence of the number is saving although closer to death.

If emotion appears—and the word seems to reappear more and more often in Opalka's discourse—it is because this passing reveals particularly his own disappearance, which is, as we know, the ultimate legitimacy of his œuvre: "My death is the logical and emotional evidence of the perfection of the œuvre." We will not argue about the association of logic and emotions, for if once again a sort of act of faith legitimized by the existential is required, again the proposition is unquestionable. Perhaps more so here since the matter is his death, past and to come. Not only because of his unistic vision, where everything would be in each thing, but because the problem is really to attest a coming death, whose temporality is indexed on a past death, a kind of symbolic death, the one that did not occur when others were dying.

Servitude, freedom, truth

It is difficult to speak about the experience of deportation, *a fortiori* since he hardly permits it to himself. That is the reason why I have chosen not to place these thoughts on the ethical condition of his œuvre in determinating relations with this moment of his life, but on the contrary to come to it when it becomes inevitable. The unquestionable, the existential evidence, the will to be beyond suspicion, all that takes on another meaning when returning from the camps. Not that the analysis should stall before such a horror liable to suspend the judgment. But there are sentences or gestures that make sense in the continuity of an experience at the same time ineffaceable and nonrepresentable. I think that the œuvre of Opalka, including OPALKA 1965/1 - ∞, is inscribed there, not exclusively but entirely. The shortness of breath, the weakness of the body, the inscription of the body in the œuvre are its products. The two stories that Opalka repeats, the one about the ball and the one of the clock, quoted at the beginning, are the discreet mythical form of that anguish of annihilation.

But there is more to it or worse. If as he recalls it, Opalka was not a victim of the Shoah, but deported as Polish, there is no reason to establish a hierarchy of horror. He was deported at the age of nine (couldn't it also be that the choking voice, when the hand that traces the numbers is in abeyance between the 9 and the 10, shows the terror of never being ten years old?). He knew solitary confinement, and his experience of the inhuman and the unmentionable had surely no need to be intensified by the suffering of Halszka whose father died at the camp of Oranienburg in 1942 (for having refused to give the

Germans a list of communist Resistance fighters). His reserve says it all: "I will say no more about what we lived through." His œuvre also.

In front of the first *Detail* of Opalka that I saw, without knowing a thing about him, then knowing his œuvre, in front of several *Details* seen together for the first time after a long interval, at the Biennal in Venice in September 1995, my first impression was the same: confusedly that it was about human numbers, that is to say numbers put in the place of names—and precisely of those numbers that had aimed actively at the negation of the human being, in the camps (I do not reconstruct this impression a posteriori, I'm one of those to whom this idea comes systematically).

The tattooed number, but without the skin and without the color of the ink. Everything grayed, save pathos, abstract, exemplary. Minus the flesh, minus the crimson tint. Neutral, in half-mourning. With the discretion of a ghost and the beauty, disembodied, but vital nevertheless, of this superb scansion on the canvas. The number of indignity divested of its unbearable pathos, and reconverted to the numeration of life.

This *double-bind* is no longer theoretical: we can see to what existential degree are indeed held the vital and the mortal in this œuvre. We can also measure the absolute necessity of all these indexes (photography, voice) directed towards the reality of the act of painting-counting, a necessity proportioned to the surprise that there still may be a possibility of counting—which invalidates the very question of monotony. This peculiar double-bind of the counting gains meaning also, advancing towards the encounter of a death that was already there nearly at the origin. Another form of alterity is also outlined: to count for the lives that don't count any more ("I think of all the children...who did not come back," an answer to Michel Nuridsany).[9] "The plotting of responsibility" takes on a more precise but incommensurable value, and one understands that it took time before undertaking a project whose title would bear his name, in capital letters, while restoring the number to its genuine function: OPALKA 1965/1 - ∞; and still a little more time before the self-portraits could make the counting literally recover human figure.

> "If we speak, they will not listen to us, and if they listen, they will not understand. They will even take away our name: and if we want to keep it, we will have to find ourselves the strength to do so, to manage somehow so that behind the name something of us, of us as we were, still remains.
> ...Clausner shows me the bottom of his bowl, where others have carved their number, and Alberto and I our names...[10]". (Primo Levi)

[9] "Face à Godot", interview with Michel Nuridsany, *Galeries Magazine*, fév. mars 1992.

[10] Primo Levi, *If this is a man*, 1957, trad. Stuart Woolf, Vintage, 1996.

The voluntariness of the Opalkian enterprise, the self-induced assertion of absolute freedom and this great turnabout of servitude, acquire their full meaning here. The concern of controllability is constant from the very conception of the project-program to the least detail of its realization—where the artist controls it all, from the height of the reflector to the percentage of white. The principle of reversal to the identical, analysed previously on the subject of penury, is here again applied to incarceration, which adopts the chosen and controlled form of technical and existential constraint. The required rule of life for what Opalka calls the conduct of the œuvre, its realization, is very constraining. Each gesture, of the artist, loaded with a personal yet universal value ("moral, philosophical and emotional gestures"), is integrated in the project. At that price, only, shall the œuvre be enabled to attest to the time of the world through the time of the artist, and pretend to show the "truth." The truth according to Opalka has the invariability of a fleeting definition, somewhat sacrificial; it is the measure of the part of life that may be sacrificed to the œuvre. In order to be the imprint of a testimony, perhaps the testimony itself, it levies its vampirish dues. His purpose is merged within the progress of his life, death included.

Death itself is subject to the most amazing reversal. The highest folly of the Opalkian project is really to perpetually foresee death. It is written from the start and permanently within the horizon of the œuvre, with its un-forseeable aspect. The care with which Opalka never interrupts his work at the end of a canvas, aims at always allowing the pictorial counting-process, so that the project may surprise death and not the reverse. And, that is perhaps where the Opalkian project is the most philosophical (Agemben: "the philosopher ...must...surprise surprise"). The ultimate reversal acts upon the event and the causality. OPALKA 1965/1 - ∞ is in itself the totality of the event, and all that may occur to the man Opalka contributes to that event. The extraordinary greatness of the œuvre lies here, to have elaborated a concept, and put in place such an artistic machine that death is compelled to be a part of it. Having lived with and having suffered, in a sense, an inflicted death that has no cause but the unspeakable, Roman Opalka has created a system of artistic causality inclined to annex its own end, to win it over to its cause. Finding an aim in the desired goal, in this way, opens the path to possible freedom. Extreme effects of a punctual servitude or "man's servitude" in the Spinozian sense, the whole Opalkian system operates on this constraint, and practices it until truth may appear, thus freedom.

Facing the elaboration of such a systemic causality, the Beckettian reference and its limits is the problem, once again. It is an important point, linked to unresolved interrogations on Opalka's positions concerning the art world. With Beckett, he and others share the same desolate background, in the neutralization, the decoloration, the whispering, as we have seen. I have also spoken of this common way of proceeding by exhaustion, underlining how Opalka's procedure is structured and paradoxically vital unlike the Beckettian emptiness. What they have in common essentially is the ethical insistence on truth, which is also what separates them radically. In his essay on "the mourning of form" in Beckett, Jean-Michel Rabaté writes:

> "The emptiness of ontology and the void of anthropology allow this ethical anxiety which is at the heart of all of Beckett's work, haunted by the absence of meaning and the duty to speak out in order to make sense in the world of men.[11]"

As regards this point, Opalka is, in a sense, beyond anxiety. Neither is there death of the form in his œuvre, and the meaning is not centered around a collapse. Beyond catastrophe, a minimal yet total form is reconstructed, in a sort of self-ontology. The irreductible originality of the œuvre, relying on the reality of his vital count-down, is his anthropological truth. One is by haunted a past of collapse and not on a constant emptiness. But, there is a common ethic, the assignment of saying and showing something that may have to do with the fact of giving oneself the assignment to say and to show.

To say and show all the same, with Beckett. To say and show again, with Opalka. Curiously, Opalka seems to be partly mistaken about the meaning of the wait with Beckett; he often quotes the play *Waiting for Godot*, integrating it with his personal vision. One of the answers given to Michel Nuridsany is, in that matter, extremely interesting. The latter asked him if other Polish artists such as Zbigniew, Gostomski or Starczewski, who also work with clasifications and systems of numbers and signs, go in this same direction.

> "Opalka: Not at all. I am someone that can be considered apart from all that happened. The others were into novelty. There is an illusion of novelty. One cannot always invent a new world...I reached a solution which enables me to wait with dignity. For the time being, solutions do not exist, but we must keep on searching. Without cheating. Not declaring that all is possible. We are like Beckett in front of Godot...You were asking me previously if I had been marked by the months of incarceration during my childhood. In fact I was more influenced by Beckett than by the ordeal I lived through, that I saw until we were liberated by the Americans in Germany. Because Godot is a universal problem."

Even considering the lack of precision inherent in every interview, his remarks show a want of logic. The replacement of the field of factual experience

[11] Jean-Michel Rabaté, *La Pénultième est morte*, Seyssel, Champ Vallon, 1993.

by that of art is another form of distantness, easily understood. All the same Opalka doubly offsets the traumatism, with first a literary transposition, Beckett, then his own artistic transposition—plastic, literary, poetic. When taken out of the context, the sentence: "I have reached a solution which enables me to wait with dignity," would evoke existential ethics and not straightaway the plastic determinations it entails. The logic of confusion is one of the elements to be taken into consideration in the analysis of Opalka's esthetic choices, actually historical, always. For the formal novelty is for him not dissociable from the the event in general, whatever happens is thus uncontrollable. Stating here contradictorily that Beckett is, beyond the contemporary period, in universal time, but that he could not have been other than contemporary, Opalka seems to define his own temporal status, according to his wishes—in his epoch, but out of time. Only his *wait* is not Beckettian: if Godot represents the meaning that is always elusive, the subject of the wait of OPALKA 1965/1 - ∞ is on the contrary this finality that can not fail to occur—ultimately and incessantly—confirming the sense of the œuvre. Is there anything less Beckettian than this Opalkian assertion: "The *Detail* in progress on the easel is, and always is, sufficiently finished, the continuous state of there is"?

Beyond catastrophe and unbearable anxiety, the ethics enable (that is an overstatement) a man to go from emptiness to livable. If the inhuman counting recovers figure, if disaster turns into project and panic to control, it is because of ethics. Reverting to the original meaning, it is also a rule, a habit, that does not govern an existing existential space but creates it.

Ethos where I remain

> "Imagine now a man who is deprived of everyone he loves, and at the same time of his house, his habits, his clothes, in short, of everything he possesses." (Primo Levi)

He rebuilds his house: he will inhabit his concept.

Roman Opalka has always looked for houses resembling him, at Mazury in Poland, from 1966 to 1986, at Bazérac in France, since 1977. Simplicity of the landscape, of the stone. Inside, the studio. The artist defined its model in 1972, to be reproduced wherever he goes, New York, Berlin, Paris, then Bazérac. Everything is organized, measured to the centimeter, the location of the spotlights, of the reflector, their height too. Standing, the painter is in the center of a veritable setting, with, facing him, a canvas his size, jutting slightly above him, of the height of the easel, and behind him, the white-clothed reflector, somewhat like symbolic walls on two sides. In the study at Mazury, the rest opens onto a staircase and the attic of this farmhouse. On the pictures I have, of that place, the beams, the steps and the rods of the banister of the staircase form a highly structured space, all around, like a powerful syntax. There is also a bed in the studio, minimal. In the studio at Bazérac, the composition of the work room is more refined. The structure is stark and sumptuous. The freestone wall, is a neutral inside-outside that enhances the autonomy of the place, its completeness. The neutral coloration of the sandy tints with the whites of the canvas, of the painter's outfit, of the reflector, the articulated silhouettes of the microphones configure the structure of the place, in the symbolic purity of their lines, black on white.

A house within the house, a space within the space, the studio of Opalka does not, nevertheless, give either the impression of imprisonment, or of protection against destruction. But on the contrary, it seems a place so highly planned, so real in its abstraction, that it may be open, symbolically of course, to the world. The artist's dertermination has created the place where he lives. The mental economy is sufficient to constitute the space. On the list of categorical injuctions which compose the great Opalkian *I Must*, is this one: "I must inhabit space as a home." The ethical imperative takes on a joyful form of assignation to a (forced) residence—meaning here, for the subject and the freedom he gives himself of occupying the space of the world, and the authorization (coming from the freedom) of remaining, in the sense of existing still.

The artist inhabits the place of his concept, he is assigned to residence. The only thing that protects the subject (and not the artist, nor the man) against catastrophe, is having constituted the place of *Ethos*. There is thus in OPALKA 1965/1 - ∞ a necessary utopian form of ethical tranquility. Anxiety is assigned to the accidental, whereas the ethical syntax—the practice of obligation—must guarantee an ontological safety. In case of accident, the assignation remains:

> "And even if we find ourselves, one day, in the situation of universal catastrophe, I will be conceptually authorized and even morally obliged to pursue my numbering until the end."

Should the whole project tend towards stating this, should the whole elaboration of the performance and of all the photographic, acoustic, pictographic indexes tend towards basing this assurance on the obligation of remaining oneself, nevertheless its scope would be limitless.

Thus the apparent split between the totally subjective and the universal is finally justified, if that was necessary. Any look upon Opalka's œuvre that would choose only one of these two poles, the extreme attention he pays to himself or the universal postulation, would miss the originality: this *mise en œuvre* of literally existential ethics, with such exemplarity that when answering for himself, the artist answers for everything. To itself its own cause and its own necessity, OPALKA 1965/1 - ∞ is this "œuvre worthy of being lived."

Opalka's Number

@ *1 Intention*

These pages will be devoted to a (summary) examination of Opalka's *Project* from a particular and very narrow viewpoint: *the notion of number.* The stated intention of the project concerns another notion, that of *time*. But time is approached through numbers; not just any numbers, whole numbers. These, above all, will be the subject here. Before speaking of time, we must speak of numbers. Without numbers, the idea of time remains too vague (it's not much clearer with them, but that's another story).

@ *2 Knowledge of the program is taken for granted*

All necessary knowledge of the project or the *program* (Opalka's word), its modalities, its protocols, is taken for granted. I will occasionally call upon what the artist himself has to say, when it touches on the particular aspect being treated. I will use what is more or less a *narrative*, a genealogy of the work in progress.

@ *3 After the Chronomes*

The transition from the project's prehistory to the *Project* was made in 1965, with the abandonment of the *Chronomes*. The stated motivation was the question of the legibility of the *arrow of time*. The points proliferating on the canvas in the *Chronomes* did not indicate the direction in which they should be read; on the contrary, the enlarging series of whole numbers advancing over the *Details* marks the progression. In both cases it is theoretically a question of the same number, the whole number, which is called the *natural* number.

@ 4 The number of the *Chronomes* was linked to what is usually considered the most archaic idea of the number. This type of number presents itself as a succession of points (the notches which can be vaguely distinguished on prehistoric mammoth tusks are the oldest surviving testimony of this idea; the vertical stripes which the prisoner or soldier inscribes on the walls of his cell or barrack-room are made according to the same principle). This idea of the representation of numbers served more than a century ago for the axiomatic definition forged by Peano.

@ 5 Peano's construction

We begin with a first number, represented by a point (or any other conventional sign fixed once and for all), and we give it a *successor*, which will be marked, represented, by adding a point at the right of the first; it can be noted as *s (.)*, for example. Then we begin again: two points, three points, like this:...The conventional "three little dots" of enumeration, as Edward Nelson recalls, are an allusion to the sequential mode of generating numbers. Following Nelson, we will call this the *genetic number*. It is held to represent the most pure form of the whole number. Its construction by the operation of succession encompasses the entire series of possible whole numbers, pushing ahead its little pebbles, points, notches, or any other unchangingly repeated signs, one by one. The Peano series of whole numbers is made entirely of "ones," all similar. And the rhizomatic spots, the drips of pictorial time, the painted "ones" that animated the *Chronomes*, were or should have been the same.

@ 6 Drawback

The idea underlying this mode of generating numbers is that of an order, a succession, a series, which is supposed to represent a discontinuous, discrete stenography of the irreversible flow of time in the direction it has taken since the Big Bang, the formidable arrow of time that the evolution of the macrocosm imposes on us, as on all the microcosm. That's exactly the role that Opalka assigned to the number, and which it fulfilled poorly in the *Chronomes*. For these, being clusters of points on a surface of canvas, indicated no direction of reading to correspond to that of inscription. The direction would have had to be introduced artificially.

@ 7 Another drawback

What is more, even if this unidirectional reading had been possible, it would not have allowed for any comprehensible way to punctuate time's passage with numbers. For to know that the point we're looking at is, say, the 53rd in the Peano series, you'd have to count again from the start. The notation of the genetic number by undifferentiated symbols imitates very well the discontinuous, *discrete* aspect of the phenomenon of time's flow (which is just one of the notion's two fundamental aspects, for time must also be conceived as *continuous*; I'll come back to that). But such notation makes it almost impossible, except in the most approximate way, to know precisely where you are.

@ 8 *The quality of the ordinary series*

The superiority of notation in figures, using the conventional series 1, 2, 3... is to avoid this drawback. It manifests the very interesting property of the genetic number, the number constructed primarily as order, which is that any element of the series, for example 17, is not only one number among others, but also designates the number of numbers which precede it. *A number serves to count the numbers leading up to it.* The number 17 is itself; it is also the seventeenth number.

@ 9 *Ordinals, cardinals*

This face of the number, which is termed *ordinal*, is what interests Opalka; not its second fundamental mask, which he calls that of measure (in reference to time), but which from the mathematical viewpoint is known as the *cardinal* aspect. The number serves to tell how much; it's an instrument allowing for an answer to the question, how many are there? To express why there are as many sheep in the flock as there are pebbles in the pile (a cherished example for historians of numeration), the whole number is there, telling us "because in each case there are *this many*"; the meaning of *this many* being expressed by a number from the series of wholes. It's a kind of little miracle that the genetic number should be capable of expressing *quantity, cardinality*, in this way. (And in fact the miracle is only performed by finite numbers).

@ 10 *Arithmetic*

This might seem to take us beyond our field of investigation, since Opalka states with utmost clarity that only the series of numbers is related to his *Project*; but it must also be said that the mathematician's interest in the genetic number stems from the fact that its simple construction as a sequence, with the small number of requisite axioms, is the basis upon which one can not only define the cardinal number, but also do arithmetic. Thus the genetic number allows us to make sense of the common operations of addition, multiplication (which is an addition repeated a given number of times), and exponentiation (which comes from multiplication multiplied in its turn); it extends even to iterated exponentiation, or hyper-exponentiation. One can consider not only the number 17 and the number 53, but also 17 + 53, 17 x 53, 17^{53} (17 to the 53rd power). The possibility of these operations, the properties of numbers they enclose in their functioning, the immense, mysterious, and difficult domain they open up—*arithmetic*—is implicit in the simple given of the series. But—and this "but" is important—the implicit must be shaken out of its implicitness. If one takes the genetic number, the series 1, 2, 3..., as the primordial given, before everything else (which is what Opalka does), then a number only "exists" if it can be constructed in this way, if it can be reached by advancing with a single step at a time, "one" by "one," on the basis of a first "one," laid down and expressed by the *figure 1*.

@ 11 Banality

The written series of numbers—which becomes a painted series in the canvases, the sequence of *Details* in Opalka's unitary program—is the series to which we're all accustomed. It seems to be of tremendous banality. Although it encloses the very secret of some of the most difficult and mysterious theorems of mathematics, like Fermat's Great Theorem which has just recently been demonstrated a good three centuries after its formulation, still on the surface it hardly appears strange to us. We have been familiar with it since childhood, since we became "numerate" (as people are said to be "literate"). The natural reaction after the presentation of a thumbnail sketch of Opalka's program—something like "he paints the series of whole numbers on his canvases"—is likely to resemble that of the high-school students led by some unfortunate Parisian teacher to London to see the Turners in the Clore Gallery, where I overheard one of them say, "This guy didn't exactly bust his brains, did he?"

@ 12 Fibonacci

Quite different would be (and generally is) the reaction to artistic undertakings which also rest on series of numbers, like the famous series of Leonardo of Pisa, known as Fibonacci. In that case, we *must* be told what it's all about; the mode of generation *must* be invoked immediately. It's relatively simple, but that doesn't suffice; we *must know* or we *must be told*, that this series is linked to the mysterious *golden section*, and thus has in itself a magical, mystical, intrinsic artistic value, not only of immense profundity in itself, but also stretching back like the Nile to remotest Antiquity, and so on... Otherwise we won't see a thing, and we won't be able to look with the necessary reverence.

@ 13 Wysiwyg, and others

In Opalka's case we see clearly and immediately what it's all about. We think we know: and we think there's nothing more to know (of course, I'm only talking about the question of numbers). Concerning the *Details* of 1965/1 - ∞ (*Infinity*), one can say *Wysiwyg*: "What you see is what you get." In the case of Fibonacci (and similars: chance numbers, series of numbers associated with the decimals of the number pi, etc.), you have to say *Wydsiwyg*: "What you don't see is what you get" (at least, that's what they say and what you must believe or hope to be true). What I'd like to bring to light here concerning Opalka's undertaking is *Ygmtwys*: "You get more than what you see," or *Timtmte*: "There is more than meets the eye." But you have to dig a little below the obvious. And the non-obvious is in fact hidden by the *radical simplicity of the project.*

@ 14 Proposals for numerical "land art": the question of fragmentation

Let's return for an instant to the *Chronomes* and the sequence of points in the "pure" construction of the genetic number. To render that visually you would either have to put a directional sign on the canvas, as I said before, or, ideally, represent the series on a single horizontal line, for example by putting big fat dots on milestones and setting them out in the landscape, at regular intervals, along Hadrian's wall, or the Great Wall of China, or even better, along the equator, beginning at the Greenwich meridian (to firmly establish the idea) and taking care not to go entirely around the earth, so as to avoid any possible confusion. In short, numerical land art. The layout of points on canvases, two dimensional and fragmented, introduces artificial breaks. But, you'll object, isn't it the same in Opalka's solution? Isn't the series of numbers as it appears in the *Details* also fragmented, and laid out in two dimensions? I will demonstrate that there is an essential difference between the two cases, but you'll have to wait a little while for that.

@ 15 A glance at the beginning

The decision to begin with the figure 1 to represent the first number of the series marks Opalka's evident impatience with another figure which could also have served, the figure representing zero (he goes so far as to call in the Greeks for reinforcement here). "I began with 1 and not with 0, just as I did not come to the idea of the counted-picture from nothing (from 0), but from the preexisting continuity of unity..." From the viewpoint of the genetic number, represented by any series of figure-signs (or other signs), there is obviously no difference between beginning with zero and beginning with one (or by -606 if it so happens); the mathematical series of numbers is indifferent to any renumeration. The motive for Opalka's choice clearly goes beyond purely numerical considerations, and thus leads outside the field of the present study; I will not discuss the reasons the artist gives for it, which could be usefully treated in another context.

@ 16 And yet

And yet let us say this: the story Opalka tells of the genesis of his *Project* shows that when he committed himself to it, it was the start of a new life; a veritable *vita nova* opening up before him. Without going any further down this path we could say that the 1 took all the future upon it, the future of both the artist's work and his life; while the 0, on the contrary, signified in a sense all the past, empty because gone.

@ 17 And yet more

Along the same line of thought, it's clear that the apprehension of the world, the ordering of the world, also comes about for children through numbers, which are linked to their apprehension of time, the arrow of time. The notion of time like the notion of number rests on that particular kind of nursery rhyme which is called a *counting rhyme*: and no counting rhyme begins with zero. In a sense, Opalka's work can be considered an immense counting rhyme. There is a clear link with the many elements which, as the painter himself stresses, relate the process to a *ritual.* For the counting rhyme is a ritual, a ritual appropriation of numbers. And one of the hypotheses put forth concerning the origin (in prehistoric times) of the naming of numbers is precisely the ritualistic hypothesis (the child's counting rhyme being in this case an example of phylogenetic recapitulation by human young). But let's remain sober.

@ 18 The royal 1

Outside the 1, which is in a kind of royalty position, it can be said that the treatment of the numbers in the series is democratic. Arithmetic has its princes, for example, the prime numbers; certain other numbers can acquire letters of nobility, or lose them over the course of the historical development of mathematics. Some numbers are fallen lords, like the perfect numbers the Pythagoreans dreamed of (6 and 28, for instance, which are equal to the sum of their divisors, excepting themselves: 6 = 3 + 2 + 1; 28 = 14 + 7 + 4 + 2 + 1). In the *Details* one sees only a series, humble and proud all at once, elementary in any case: numbers which are all equal in value, which have all received equal care, if not equal expense of paint and brush strokes. If they do not remain equal *in fact*, it is because a few step out of rank in the course of the work's progress; but the fact that this access to pictorial notoriety is strictly the result of their generative process and of what the artist lives through as he brings them to visible existence is an important event for the very meaning of the project. Here I will allow myself a significant quotation.

@ 19 An interest invented as you go along

"It's a matter of an interest invented as you go along, if you observe these repetitions and differences in all their appearances since the beginning of the progression: from 22 to 666666... multiple appearances and apparent disappearances in the numbers composed—a labyrinthine relation—all the way to the final and unique limit-repetition of these seven signs: 1111111. These numerical rendezvous crop up throughout the progression after each passage of millions, in more and more distant meetings between the first two and 2222222 as well as all the other encounters of this nature, from the first 7 to the last 7777777 which closes the series of 7 identical signs..."

@ 20 Totality, infinity

From the very beginning, in 1965, as the general title of "work in progress" indicates, it was a matter of painting a *totality* of numbers, the totality of numbers; it was a matter of providing *a painted image of infinity*. At the basis of the project there is the idea of a "founding totality." Each detail of each *Detail* only makes sense in relation to this totality: "Each detail bears the dynamics of the totality."

@ 21 To be sure, infinity is unattainable

It's clear to everyone that infinity is unattainable. By dint of stubborn and continuous application, the program will attain (and already has attained) a very large number, to be sure—but never infinity. Opalka does not claim the contrary. He advances toward infinity with the series of numbers, which can always be prolonged, which can always be augmented with a new unit. This is the characteristic "plus one" of the potential infinity created by the genetic number, as in those battles between children who have just learned their numbers and who play at who'll say the largest: "a million" says one, "ten million," says the other, "a hundred million," even "a thousand billion billion billion"—until one finally discovers the decisive argument that stops the whole battle by showing that neither can win: "plus one." (I can still hear the *più uno* of such a dispute in an Italian neo-realist film, *Miracle in Milan*.)

@ 22 Giving something to be seen, in thought

But Opalka has found a way to give this infinity to be seen in thought, and it must be admitted that it's a quite extraordinary way, no doubt without equal in the history of art:

> "My project will end in its own incompletion. If I die today, this work of numeration which tends toward infinity and therefore knows no other limit than my human life span, will logically find its completion in its very unfulfillment. Thus this unfinishedness becomes the finality of my work, and that is a unique situation in the history of art: *I define the finite by the unfinished*" (my emphasis—J.R.).

@ 23 Georg Cantor's invention

Now, on the one hand, a characteristic of the *infinite genetic potential* is its *radical incompletion*. One can only count the finite. One can not reach beyond. But since Cantor, mathematics has decided to deal with *actual infinity*, to give it a status, to reason with it as though it were real. Or rather, against the entire tradition since Aristotle, to affirm its mathematical reality. This affirmation was made manifest by Cantor's intervention, a gesture of writing which placed a new number at the very end of the series of natural numbers: the well-named *omega,* the first *transfinite* number.

@ 24 An allegory

In his allegory of the finite and the infinite, of the ephemeral, the fleeting, and the eternal, Opalka has inscribed an irrefutable translation of Cantor's omega: the instant, the "number" of his own death, which no series of figures in any system of numeration can put down on a sheet of paper, a computer screen, or a canvas, without leaving "as many" empty places as those it has been possible to fill (the terrifying property of actual infinity). All the series of the *Details*, the *Travel Maps*, the enormous labor of so many years, is pointed toward what can be called *an infinity for all practical ends*. It is not only because the number that will finally be attained is great; its magnitude is relative, larger ones can be spoken, larger ones can be written, can be calculated, conceived, imagined; but it is larger than all those that have ever been traced by the *hand of man,* as a *number in a genetic series*, that is to say, a number coming after all those others which have been actually put down. It is likely that no larger such number will ever be written. It brings us as close as we can imaginably come to the infinite, in so far as the infinite is *inaccessible* to man alone.

@ 25 Let us reflect

Let us reflect on the fact that the number we are considering here is a kind of number which is constructed step by step. Each number "proves its existence" by coming immediately after those which have already been constructed, or gone through. One must not skip any number in the series. From this point of view, whether you count or you paint, it takes an awfully long time to reach a big number (the first no doubt goes much quicker than the second, but the problem is the same). From this point of view, if you consider "one billion" for example, we are in a situation of *quasi-infinity*. Where one-by-one construction is concerned, 1 and "one billion" are *incommensurable*: a billion is quasi-infinitely larger than 1.

@ 26 Cantor's trump card

Under these conditions it's clear that to accept (as Cantor and mathematics after him have done) the "reality" of the set of all the whole numbers and to give it a limit, omega, is to add a trump card to the deck. To affirm the actual existence of *n*, the complete set of numbers, is to indirectly affirm the *real existence of eternity*. From this point of view, potential infinity—the one said not to exist in totality, but to be a finite number that can always be augmented—is but a *timid infinity*. Why not immediately face omega and all its successors, the tribe of the *transfinites*? When moving towards omega in the genetic series, it is said to be always possible, wherever one arrives, to go farther, to add one more, to say *più uno*. Okay. But what does "always" mean? In fact, if we consider actual enumeration, whether it's a child counting, a computer printing numbers one by one, or Opalka in his *Details*, none of them will ever go farther than they go; and wherever they go will always remain a finite number. Never will anything but the finite be reached in a constructive way, "one by one." You can conceive infinity and infinities of vaster and vaster size, you can reason correctly about them, "justify" them by more and more sophisticated logical systems, but you can never build on anything but the finite. As a construction, Cantor's infinity is just finitude in disguise.

@27 Strange, strange

The question is apparently very simple. You construct a genetic series which cannot be completed; Cantor completes it with a new, "transfinite" number, omega. In effect it is known that if one represents the whole numbers in their succession by points on a straight line, and if one puts new numbers between them, representable as fractions, one can not exhaust the numbers which can thus be placed *between*; and the problem of the infinite appears again, in its relations with time, at least since Zeno of Elaia. But in fact, the question of the relations of finitude and infinity is, for mathematics and logic today, much stranger. Finitude and infinity are far more tangled up with each other than had been imagined. For different logicians and mathematicians in the course of this century, the infinite has presented a welter of far more vexing problems. Let's take an example from the domain of poetry.

@ 28 Cmmp

In 1961, a French poet, novelist, and mathematician named Raymond Queneau published a book of poetry entitled *Cent mille milliards de poemes* ("One hundred thousand billion poems"). The principle of this book was quite simple. Queneau had composed ten sonnets, each of fourteen verses. These sonnets were written in such a way that it was possible to compose a new sonnet, which would be grammatically correct, present proper rhymes, contain verses of the right meter, and make sense, by taking any one of the first verses from the original sonnets and following it by any one of the second verses, and so on all the way to the fourteenth. A simple calculation shows that the poems "potentially" produced in this way numbered "ten to the fourteenth power," 10^{14} in exponential notation, that is, sure enough, one hundred thousand billion. And Queneau noted in his preface that "counting 45 seconds to read a sonnet, and 15 to [construct] another, at a rate of eight hours a day, 200 days a year, there will be enough for more than a million centuries of reading." Which is quite a lot.

@ 29 Nelson intervenes

Now I'm going to slightly paraphrase a quotation from Nelson (Edward, the logician, not the admiral; the sentences I will quote appear in a very austere book entitled *Predicative Arithmetic*; Nelson is not a poet, nor a philosopher, nor a physicist; but he is someone very serious). I modify the text just slightly to adapt it to the context of Queneau's *Cmmp*, supposing, to make the example even clearer, that the number of poems is 50.

> *"We postulate an entity, the set of all possible printed poems, and then we ascribe some kind of reality to this entity—for example, by asserting that one can in principle read each possible poem. But perhaps it is simply not so. Perhaps there no such number as 10^{50}; perhaps it is always possible to write a new and different poem. Many ordinary activity are built up in a similar way from a rather small set of symbols or actions. Perhaps infinity is not far off in space or time or thought; perhaps it is*

while engaged in an ordinary activity—writing a page, getting a child ready for school, talking with someone, teaching a class, making love—that we are immersed in infinity."

@ 30 Nelson's objection

Without entering upon the difficult and perhaps vain discussion of the "degrees of reality" of numbers, according to their mode of generation, let us say that what Nelson wants to insist on in this passage is that we should always remember that numbers are not given entities mysteriously put at our disposal once and for all, as if fallen from "the great empyrean sky," as Claude de Kaerlec said in the 15th century. When we speak of numbers and reason about them, we must know very precisely how they were constructed. Nelson himself pleads for a *formal* construction of the number. The genetic number doesn't satisfy him. I quote:

> "*Why are mathematicians so convinced of the fact that exponentiation* [the operation invoked by Queneau] *is total* [that is, that all the expressions that can be written with the operation really exist]*? Because they believe in the existence of abstract objects called numbers....*
>
> "*What is a number? Originally, sequences of tally marks were used to count things....*
>
> "*Then positional notation* [the kind used by Opalka, the kind we all use]—*the most powerful achievement of mathematics* [linked to the discovery of the zero, not as a symbol of emptiness, but as an instrument of notation]—*was invented... It has been universally assumed, on the basis of scant evidence, that decimals are the same kind of things as sequences of tally marks* [the points of the *Chronomes*, for example], *only expressed in a more practical and efficient notation. This assumption is based on a semantic view of mathematics, in which mathematical expressions, such as decimals and sequences of tally-marks, are regarded as denoting abstract objects ...*
>
> "*But to one who takes a formalist view of mathematics, the subject matter of mathematics is the expressions themselves together with the rules for manipulating them—nothing more. From this point of view, the invention of positional notation was the creation of a* new kind of number (my emphasis—J. R.)....
>
> "*Mathematicians have always operated on the unchallenged assumption that it is possible in principle to express 10^{50} as a numeral by performing the recursively indicated computations....*
>
> "*To say that it is possible in principle is to say that the recursion will terminate in a certain number of steps—and this use of the word 'number' can only refer to the primitive notion: the steps are things that are counted by a sequence of tally marks. In what number of steps will the recursion terminate? Why, in somewhat more than 10^{50} steps. The circularity in the argument is glaringly obvious....*

"The difference between the formal and genetic construction is the difference between sitting confortably in camp and saying, 'if I have climbed part way up the mountain, then I can take one more step up the mountain', and actually climbing a mountain, when each successive step requires an act."

@ 31 Opalka's number

The parallel between Nelson's approach and that of Opalka is striking. Leaving behind the domain of the arithmetic number, or of the various kinds of arithmetic numbers, we are in the presence of a different type of number, numbers written genetically, but actually written one by one, and in a particular way which is perfectly and explicitly defined (we know how carefully Opalka indicates the very regular procedure which he employs to *define*—as we will henceforth say—a number of the type he creates, the *painted whole number*).

@ 32 Very big numbers

We must now reconsider the notion of the *very big number*; and with this, a second characteristic of the *program* will take on a new meaning.

@ 33 The idea of distinction

If one recalls the idea of number which underlies the genetic definition, namely step-by-step construction, one realizes that the larger the numbers of this type become, the less clearly and distinctly are they defined—for they are very far away in the series, very difficult to attain. Their drawbacks from the viewpoint of arithmetic are very serious. For example, there is no problem in conceiving the number 10^{14}, except for the difficulty of actually counting up to it from the number 1. One clearly "sees," in thought, where this number is to be found in the sequence, and one can easily write it in positional notation, which indicates the steps to be taken in order to reach it: 1, followed by fourteen zeros. But what about the number 9^{15}, which is 9 multiplied by itself 15 times? What is its genetic face, the only one which can grant it reality, according to this conception of number? Computers, perhaps, will tell us; but they will not tell us *what* the genetic number represented as the result of the sum $17^{53} + 53^{17}$ can be. From this point of view the very big numbers are struck with arithmetic awkwardness, if not powerlessness.

@ 34 Count again

That's not all. Suppose you tell me: "Here's the number 8888888, I counted it." I answer back: "Really? Let's have a look at this. Can you count it again please?"

@ 35 Indistinct numbers

The difficulty of reaching these dinosaurs, their gravity and awkwardness, the obstacles to any manipulation of these pachyderms, makes the very big numbers less and less distinct members of the genetic family, to the point where they are finally indistinct numbers. That's why one can only be struck, anew, by the fact that even if the central decision in 1972 to gradually whiten the *Details* is essentially linked to the prediction of their completion in incompletion (perfect, absolute white being in principle, though not in practice, unattainable by the chosen procedure), still the decision implies a concrete realization of this fact: the very big numbers tend toward indistinctness, anonymity, invisibility. The diminution of the gray, the invasion of white, is also theoretically infinite, like the genetic series itself: if 1% is taken away, something always remains, ideally anyway (it converges toward zero, but never reaches it, except practically).

@ 36 Accessory remarks

The moment when the paint shines before disappearing on the white ground resembles the infinitely short trajectories of particles in microphysics. At one moment, as whiteness is approached, the vision of the canvases becomes an experience of thought.

@ 37 Errors

Also important in this perspective is the fact that Opalka has never fallen into the trap of strict correction, the faultless repair of the occasional errors. What he constructs is an image-sequence of the genetic number, and it is a concrete sequence, with its inevitable imperfections.

@ 38 The idea of speeds of access

One could thus postulate the "existence" of weaker and weaker numbers as one progresses through the "natural" series. The big numbers are less and less whole (by their indistinctness, inaccessibility, anonymity). One could then compare the numbers between each other by speeds of access. Genetic access is walking: you go step by step. Addition, multiplication, exponentiation, and hyperexponentiation are trains: omnibus, express, inter-city, high speed (TGV). In other words, we have many ways of progressing through the series of numbers; and they allow for highly variable speeds.

@ 39 Languages come into the picture

Here is where languages come into the picture. Take for example 53: I reach it in 53 steps (let's say it's omnibus speed; I stop at every number-station).

However, I could act differently 10, 20, 30, 40, 50, 51, 52, 53, in eight "jumps" (express plus omnibus); and for all of us, the whole number reached by the second procedure is no less "certain" than the one reached by the first, the canonical procedure. Indeed, we implicitly possess, as a kind of numerical second nature, a certainty that is founded on our way of counting, of counting in words. It could of course be said that this certainty is of lower quality; and in case of doubt, for sufficiently large numbers, we'd have to go back to the omnibus, or go by foot; take stakes, and drive them one by one into the ground along the path. Yet human history shows that in each language, ways of speeding up the counting process have been devised. With the risk, when the numbers become very big, of exceeding the limits of what is really possible: the delirium of saying "a billion billion billion." One could then distinguish the speeds of access to numbers according to the type of vehicle employed. There is language, which speaks the numbers. There is writing, which notes them in a more condensed way. One can also distinguish human counting processes, by hand, from those of computers; and from logical constructions (the formal systems), and so on. It's easy to see that each of the operations carried out on numbers — addition, multiplication, ordinary or iterated exponentiation — defines increasingly rapid means, accelerations of the attempt to master the big numbers.

@ 40 Slow-downs

Now, the explicit writing of the genetic numbers in decimal notation obviously advances more and more slowly. It takes much longer to write a number of seven figures than one with only six. *Opalka's number* has a particularity which is also symbolic of the totality of his project. As he approaches the inaccessible, he advances more and more slowly (and one could draw a parallel between this fact and the inevitable consequences of the inscription not simply in time, but in lived time, *durée*: the hand that traces the figures grows older).

@ 41 Spoken numbers

The same phenomenon of slow-down is at work in the diction of the numbers. But in language, because of the principles of numeration that it adopts, this slowdown is obviously unequal. There are threshold numbers, a hundred thousand, a million, and so on, which can be said much more quickly than the intermediary numbers. It's striking that when he gives voice to his numbers, Opalka has chosen, as it seems to me anyway, to maintain a clear parallel between the two time spans: that of the painted (rather than written) number and that of the spoken number which accompanies it (the commentary on the transition to the first million makes this very clear). Thus we can be even more precise about the nature of the number we are describing: *Opalka's number is a neighbor of the genetic number, painted and spoken by him.*

@ 42 Spoken, but how?

The close link between sound and painted sign in this version of the number appears even more clearly in what I will call the affair of the *nonante*. In effect, the different languages have their particular way of naming numbers, each of which resembles no other. Opalka speaks his numbers in Polish; and at the important moment when, on the verge of the first million, he prepared to paint and to speak what we read as 999999, he was led to remark, in the commentary given in French, that the French language is inadequate to render what's happening, because the French number *quatre-vingt-dix,* unlike the Polish word, covers up the "nine" which must be present in the *spoken* as well as the *seen*. For this reason he proposed the dialect variant *nonante*. From this we can immediately deduce the element that completes our final definition: *Opalka's number is a neighbor of the genetic number, painted and spoken by him in Polish.*

@ 43 Slightly backtracking

I'll backtrack for a moment to a question which I left open almost at the beginning. The separation of the work as a whole into the *Details*, and in them, the separation of the numbers into lines, introduces a fragmentation into the genetic sequence of numbers, which seems to run counter to the intention, forming an arbitrary accumulation of breaks. This is not at all true if one understands the number as it has just been expressed. Indeed, it is a fact of the naming of numbers in all languages that the sequence of their names is naturally fragmented. The fact (to remain at the most elementary level) that one says *vingt et un* in French marks a necessary fragmentation in the series, which is grouped by bunches of composite words using only a limited number of elementary names. Without such a procedure, a person counting in his own language would have no greater mastery over the sequence than over the series of undifferentiated points. (There is a Borges story where a character, perhaps scandalized by this theoretical laxity, this linguistic impurity, decides to give all the numbers different names, with no relation between them.) It follows that independently of the obvious pragmatic considerations, Opalka's number *had to be* fragmented into units, marking at once the regularity (the size of the canvases, the figures, their spacing) *and* a regulated irregularity (resulting from their slowly growing length).

@ 44 It's time to ask the question of time

Having marked an appropriate separation with all that precedes, it is time, indeed, to ask *the question of time*. Opalka's project has to do, in an essential way, with time. Here I will call upon a few fragments taken from the reflection on time, numbers, and mathematics by one of the geniuses of this century, long contested and poorly known, but more and more important for logical and mathematical thought today: the Dutchman, Luitzen Egbertus Jan Brouwer. Brouwer begins with the idea that numbers, and mathematics as a whole, must find their source in the *intuition of time*. The nature of time as it emerges from this intuition is double: it is at once *continuous* and *discrete*. The departure point of any construction must reflect this idea, whose origin is found in a *Primordial Intuition*, that of "two-in-one," which gives birth to original "two-oneness." This is the basis on which everything must be created by the mind, which thinks mathematics and creates it from this thought. This way of conceiving mathematics is has been called *intuitionism* by its inventor. Let's give him the floor for a moment:

@ 45 Brouwer:

"Intuitionism considers the falling apart of moments of life into qualitatively different parts, to be reunited only while remaining separated by time in the fundamental phenomenon of the human intellect, passing by abstraction from its emotional context into the fundamental phenomenon of mathematical thinking, the intuition of the bare two-oneness....

"The intuition of two-oneness, the basal intuition of mathematics, creates not only the numbers one and two, but also all finite ordinal numbers, inasmuch as one of the elements of the two-oneness, may be thought of as a new two-oneness, which process may be repeated indefinitely; this gives rise still further to the smallest infinite ordinal number omega....

"This basic intuition of mathematics, in which the connected and the separate, the continuum and the discrete are united, gives rise immediately to the intuition of the linear continuum, i.e. of the 'between' which is not exhaustible by the interposition of new units and which therefore can never be thought of as mere collection of units....

"In the Primordial Intuition of two-oneness the intuitions of continuous and discrete meet: 'first' and 'second' are held together, and in this holding-together consists the intuition of the continuous (continere = hold together)....

The Continuous

"The basic intuition of mathematics (and of every intellectual activity) is that the substratum, divested of all quality, of any perception of change, is a unity of continuity and discreteness, a possibility of thinking together several entities,

connected by a 'between,' which is never exhausted by the insertion of new entities. Since continuity and discreteness occur as inseparable complements, both having equal rights and being equally clear, it is impossible to avoid one of them as a primitive entity, trying to construe it from the other one, the latter being put forward as self-sufficient; in fact it is impossible to consider it as self-sufficient. Having recognised that the intuition of continuity, of 'fluidity,' is as primitive as that of several things conceived as forming together a unit, the latter being at the basis of every mathematical construction, we are able to state properties of the continuum as a 'matrix of points to be thought of as a whole'....

"But neither the act of construction, nor the concepts can be entirely detached from the creating Subject, and a mathematical concept can not be separated from the act that brought it into existence. The Subject is not solely a stonemason, nor a father who has given birth to an independent being; the mathematical object only remains alive in thought, and in conscious thought....

"Man has a faculty which accompanies all his interactions with nature, a faculty of viewing his life mathematically, seeing in the world repetitions of sequences, causal systems in time. The fundamental phenomenon here is no more than the intuition of time, which makes repetition of 'things-in-time-and-again-thing' possible and on the basis of which moments of life fall apart as sequences of qualitatively different things; these are subsequently concentrated in the intellect as mathematical sequences, not sensed but perceived....

"Since in the Primordial Intuition, *the continuous and the discrete appear as inseparable complements, each with equal rights and equally clear, it is impossible to avoid one as a primitive entity, and construct it from the other, posited as the independent primitive....*

"In the first constructive act there are two though-together discrete things...(Some) say that one *thing is sufficient since I can add a second thing the fact that I think it. This is incorrect since precisely the* adding to it *(i.e. positing while retaining what was thought before)* presupposes the intuition of two *and this mathematical structure is only afterwards applied to the original thing as thought and to the I who thinks it....*

"We recognize that the continuum intuition, the 'fluid,' is as elemental as the thinking-together of more things into one."

@ 46 Opalka's intuitionist art

As soon as I read what the artist had to say about his project, I set myself the following hypothesis: even taking account of the different aims (mathematical on one hand, artistic on the other), there is a deep relation between Brouwer's approach and that of Opalka; this is why I was tempted to qualify the latter as intuitionist. This led me to inquire how the fundamental twoness of the continuous and the discrete—which rests, in mathematical intuitionism, on the the essential relation of *between*—could be inscribed in the program.

But it jumped out immediately before my eyes. I quote the characteristic phrase: "[The] spaces between the numbers [are] of a length little different than that occupied by the numbers themselves"; these spaces offer an alternative sequence, perfectly distinct but undifferentiated. The set of painted numbers and painted spaces between those numbers is an *image* not only of infinity, finitely approached and incomplete, but also of the very duality of the continuous and the discrete.

@ 47 Halos

What is more, in the gray and increasingly white "between-numbers," one can read the crowd of temporal events close to each number, which constitute the *halo* of infinitely near numbers, their *mute shadow*. ("Halo" is an expression from the recent "non-standard analysis" which has provided a solid conceptual status to the infinitely small numbers of which Leibniz dreamed, numbers which had long been banished from the mathematical city. Of course it is a matter, not of "really" infinitely small numbers, but of quasi-infinitely small numbers, infinitely small "for all practical ends." Let's also note that the intervals, which form a silent "Peano sequence," are indeed constituted of identical symbols.)

And let's quote Opalka, speaking precisely of the "between"—in the voice, and in the advancing movement of painting—and of the silences associated with the shadow-sequence of the intervals, itself silent:

> "The most marked 'stops' in the sound-description come... from my own determination to retain the greatest possible consistency for painting: thus all these parts of the process, though not inscribed and not said in the numerical progression, describe time, between the numbers, by the silences and by all the noises which 'cut through' them..."

@ 48 Portraits

But what about the photographs of the artist associated with certain numbers? What are these faces of Opalka which punctuate the progression of the sequence? What is signified, for example, by this photograph which accompanies the writing of a certain number on the canvas, 4691337? It can be considered a moment of the project, a two-dimensional cut of the four-dimensional being Opalka, at the instant 4691337, a portrait of the author at that instant. Beyond any doubt. But I would like to propose another reading of this same document.

It is a portrait of Opalka's Number 4691337.

Its name is 4691337, and its face is the face of Opalka at the instant when the number of born, for it is indeed born, fallen into the world with the paint pouring from the brush.

A crowd of such numbers have had their portrait, no doubt for the first and only time.

Having suddenly seen it that way, afterwards I found it difficult to believe that no one had ever thought to do the pictorial portrait of numbers, as mathematicians do their mathematical portrait. And yet it's the case.

@ 49 What to conclude?

What to conclude? Nothing, probably. Except perhaps this, not as a conclusion but a coda.

Roman Opalka will have done all that a man can imagine as the most immense effort to approach the idea of the infinite, of the infinite in the finitude of time, by non-discursive, non-mathematical, irreducibly personal means, but at the same time, means given to us all.

A monument.

Opalka's Details

22 April 1985

life begins without knowing that it has hence its fondness for illusion you need to stop and work your way into time and understand it's all going to end and that end determines our existence so here now is the start of a beginning which repeats the moment of origin and at the same time doesn't repeat it because in addition it contains the successive sequence of days and it's not just a matter of not forgetting death but of seeing a possibility of plenitude opening up before you it's not an escape it's a way into the very matter of the day the artist is at work shoulders and skull in the light and behind him a spotlamp mounted on a stand which also carries a camera and a kind of open square white umbrella in front of him his picture on an easel painter and picture stand facing each other the room with its ochre stone walls and matching carpet is filled with similarly coloured air or silence in his left hand a pot of white paint in his right a brush which paints three eight zero three zero five seven in white on the gray background this number begins a new line below a multitude of others which fill three quarters of the picture's surface the right hand poised at the end of the forearm working at chin height holding the brush between thumb and fore finger all the painter's equipment is certainly there all the right postures too but what comes out of them is not what you'd expect the edge of the right hand presses against the canvas leaps a short way forwards with a slight rubbing sound the brush handle wiggles the hand goes out of sight behind the torso which suddenly swivels round what is art says the painter turning away from the picture it's not a space to act like an earnest cow in as Nietzsche used to say but a place in which to draw up an honest account with yourself my existence bears the name Opalka and so does my work I was a painter I wanted to do something with a more committed link between life and art than painting something where expression would be more important than painting

I think I am one of the few to have thought about the crazy rush towards novelty that drives the avant-garde as if it were always possible to do better or rather as if surprise were the supreme value we are too full of illusions tomorrow is just another day what I decided to do is decided once and for all I can't improve on it there's just one date 1965 the year I began there will only be one other which I don't yet know between the two the life and work of Opalka the succession and continuity of *details* each a complete and perfect object in itself I've realised it's impossible to do better that's not pretension just logic and I've structuralised it you need to understand my thinking I had made up my mind not to say anything about it but people are too busy to work it out for themselves too busy to meditate on logic and its fascination when you look at an Opalka you are looking at an impeccable piece of logic you might tell yourself it isn't much but you have to recognise at least that the thing is true that you are faced with a truth while talking Opalka has moved forwards a little he walks over to the fireplace in the middle of the right-hand wall the narrow mantelpiece is where he keeps his supply of white paint he pours a little into his pot stirs it with the brush while walking back to his canvas which is the *detail* in progress with a surface like very pale ruffled water three million eight hundred and three thousand one hundred and sixty one he says his skull and back in the light his right hand raised the current line is at mouth level glistening it joins the corner of the mouth to the tip of the thumb the hand drops down disappears a clicking sound indicates that it is dipping the brush in the pot still held by the left hand Opalka lets out a long sigh the bent head comes back up at the same time as the right hand the movement is like writing when the line is finished Opalka comes towards the left his leather jacket creaks the umbrella reflector hides the head hides the upper hand all that remains visible is the shadow of the brush on the wrist the whole hand reappears the tip of the thumb moves like a tiny snout nibbling the torso swivels the face appears in the full light with its halo of hair I carry my concept with me I've decided on it for the whole of my existence for me it's the idea that fits life best a sfumato of our limitations I am always hard at work and I can talk endlessly about my concept just as one can talk endlessly about life I wanted to change everything through my painting but I realised you can't do that I'm constantly producing novelty the real sort my work expresses a definite distance in space and time just like in nature absolutely no reversibility at my first exhibition in Milan people thought they were multiple copies of the same picture always the same distance between pictures twenty centimetres the span of my right hand an identical hanging at every exhibition people exclaim I've seen that before which is true and not true my *details* are identical and different they make that crucial fact visible I too am always the same yet never the same it's the way everything is but you can't see it every *detail* carries the trace of time you find it in Pollock too but there's nothing you can say about it his path is chaotic and time can only be read in a linear fashion a clock doesn't show time it just tells us what the time is I am very rational a mystic of rationality the hands are in front of the waist one holding the brush the other the paintpot they haven't moved they disappear when the body swivels back towards the canvas it is as if Opalka were retracting his face again the skull and shoulders seem never to have moved outside the light of their unruffled duration the right hand has settled itself vertically on the wrist-joint it swallows a little space between thumb and forefinger the brush hardly twitches Opalka turns abruptly I get my canvasses made near Turin I know that they won't vary by as much as a centimetre or even a millimetre he's the only one I can trust I've worked out the size one metre ninety-six by one thirty-five based on my height a bit like calculating skis for a specific person also with an eye to stairs doors lifts I wanted to avoid any aesthetic considerations i.e. anything not determined by the truth of proportion my picture corresponds to my body and the spread of my arms if I were an American I'd probably be a bit bigger everything's bigger in America even the bread rolls the first time I went over there on a grant it was impossible to convert my centimetres to inches I could feel there was something wrong my canvasses were too small by oh just a few millimetres in fact they were too big but the general scale of things gave the opposite impression as for the height of the figures I fixed it by thinking of someone reading them from not too close up writing always has its natural size

23 April 1985

it was in 1972 that I began the process of adding an extra one percent of white to the background of each new *detail* working towards white on white why not before because I needed a certain amount of experience to work out how many canvasses I could do in my lifetime I took the average life expectancy in the West and then I had to learn my trade it was quite new it took me seven months to paint the first *detail* the one in the Lodz gallery after five or six years I was managing to paint ten a year I have to take eye strain and tired legs into account I've had to fight Jacob's fight with the Angel to accept my decision and live with it all my life I had achieved a certain amount of success particularly with engraving won international prizes I was even being spoilt by the system of privileges for the elite I was full of doubts I wasn't sure I'd made the right decision I would stop work for two or three weeks but as soon as I put the canvas back on the easel a kind of magic happened I had heart problems and it was hard for me to stand for long periods I thought this work was going to destroy me physically I accepted the possibility and that cured the heart trouble I felt better in myself and I started to hope I'd be able to carry my plan through to the end the white I started with a black background and white figures then I switched to gray not because it was more suitable but because I liked it and deliberately because it is close to what I call truth when the one percent idea came to me I began recording myself speaking the numbers as I went along preparing the ground for the white on white the voice will tell me where I have got to because there will be nothing to see and it will also be proof that I have actually done what is no longer visible in case people don't believe me given my own scepticism about myself my work is intended to demonstrate a certain human quality my thinking is based not on faith but on knowledge Saint Augustine said you must believe in order to know I prefer it the other way round it's true in the same way a window is true Opalka is holding brush and pot his right cheek was parallel to the picture when he started to speak then his whole right side a few words later he had completely turned his back on it now he swivels round to face it again while the brush clicks away in its pot the hand rises settles the tip of the thumb edges along three million eight hundred and three thousand two hundred and twenty seven the hand disappears behind the body more clicking the current line shows up as a slight notch in the perfect expanse that has already been completed a hard edge the hand moves up again hiding the edge working away preceded by its shadow which quivers along the lighter curve around its border if you follow the line you see a narrow space advancing by tiny movements if you watch the hand it is a minutely-quivering nest which seems not to affect what is underneath it if you look at the whole surface and hand and head and body is this not a painter at work on his canvas there is something here in process of being represented something which passes from the painter's body to the surface three million eight hundred and three thousand two hundred and thirty eight he announces and this information links the moment corresponding to its utterance this moment on the twenty third of April nineteen eighty-five to the multitude of earlier moments on which it builds and which go back to that other moment in nineteen sixty-five when on a similar but black canvas was written the number one what is three million eight hundred and three thousand two hundred and thirty eight if you think about all the other numbers that had to be drawn before its seven figures could be written and are all these successive figures not the content of the latest the content therefore of its representation but what is a representation that represents nothing except the sum total of an invisible journey pursued day after day wait a minute says Opalka turning round suddenly with that abruptness of interruption which always comes as a surprise let me show you something he puts brush and pot down on the corner of the mantelpiece then opening the doors of the large glass-fronted cabinet takes out a wooden box marked armagnac vieux in black and 1931 in red ah I think to myself the year he was born he slides open the lid and the box turns out to be full of brushes little brushes all identical O Rowney S 40 Kolinsky Sable made in England all with their bristles protected by a tiny transparent tube and all with the words Opalka 1965 detail followed by very different sets of figures written lengthways in white paint on the handle you know 1965 is the date when the concept began and progression is the only thing that gives us an idea of time the calendar can express measure but not duration how can you date a *detail* while it's still in progress I designate them by the first and last number when I finish one I start the next straight away because if I have a heart attack it's important that my last *detail* should not be finished by me but by my life Opalka hands me the box and brushes and returns to the fireplace he washes his brushes in a glass of water put there for the purpose then grasps the pot but instead of going over to the picture to resume his confrontation and the transposition of his life into the figured surface he advances brush and pot in hand just imagine the emotion in the phonetic and visual transition from nine hundred and ninety nine thousand nine hundred and ninety nine to one followed by six zeros the change from six nines to six zeros is just as violent and astonishing as the change from green to red things relate to each other as much through their differences as their logical connections there were other emotional moments three threes four fours six sixes six hundred and sixty six thousand six hundred and sixty six that was in a drawing and it happened in Milan that day I realised that to get from six sixes to seven sevens would take me thirty years anyone watching me might imagine it's terrifyingly monotonous but within this apparent monotony there is extraordinary emotion it took me several years to reach one million and when I announced it my voice was terribly tense in my work there are emotional situations which would be impossible in any other creative activity emotions where the physical and intellectual commitment is like walking to the ends of the earth it's that logic that gives me the strength to continue anyone who tries to understand me can feel the same kind of emotion my *detail* is an object which gives off an energy you can feel each of my pictures has all the others in it one Bonnard isn't all the other Bonnards if I think about the black which has been painted and the white which hasn't yet it changes the one I'm looking at it isn't just what I see Opalka plunges his brush into the pot stirs it round the bottom with a rapid clicking sound there is an emotional aspect to this work so many hidden emotions which you need to rediscover and explore in order to understand the intellectual process which has led to its making to have collected and kept all the brushes you see in this box might have seemed pretentious before but after twenty years it's possible to try to understand what I'm doing retrospectively I used the same brush for all the early *details* but it got worn and made the numbers hard to read especially the eights with their two loops that mustn't be filled in so I took the decision to use a new brush for each new *detail* Opalka goes back over to the fireplace washes his brush again the box has remained open with the black handles lined up in the bottom and their white inscriptions OPALKA 1965/1 –∞ detail 3502875 3519633 OPALKA 1965/1 –∞ detail 3429223 3445207 the metal bits holding the bristles onto the handle gleam beneath the transparent covers seventeen brushes make up the top layer impossible to see how many others there are the earliest brushes have been lost Opalka says his head now seeming to emerge from the light to the left of the hand animated by a little static quivering the hand disappears to go and dip the brush the head bows at the same time and rises again following the hand which soon reaches the edge Opalka moves immediately to the left of the canvas he makes a little scratching noise with his hand I'm trying to get the border right the line isn't the same thickness all along probably because some of it was wetter the paint runs thicker after the brush has been dipped since when did the lines of a book seem monotonous to the reader's eye here the lines quickly blur in a horizontal direction which the eye only manages to re-establish in the current picture in the neighbourhood of the most recently painted line in the finished pictures the horizontal dimension at first glance is imperceptible and even close scrutiny fails to establish it I meant to tell you something that occurred to me Opalka has spoken these words facing the picture he turns round I am now the only creative artist who if the outbreak of atomic war were announced could still go on painting I can't imagine anyone else carrying on to do one more line one more shape whereas for me it's the only thing to do because of the concept when I heard my father had died I immediately set to work what I do is a record of work it's always work but it's also something else we always regard work as something external to life in my case life is work Opalka turns back to the picture his hand is three quarters of the way along the line in progress what number three million eight hundred and three thousand three hundred and fifty four he says upon which he turns away from the picture my white he says is perhaps the sound of a saxophone or perhaps as someone pointed out the white of an atomic explosion I say that to explain why I could continue working after the outbreak of atomic war he returns to the picture the skull is fully in the light pink on top beneath the white hair the corner of the right lens of his glasses makes a bright indentation in the profile the hand takes a tiny leap Opalka sighs deeply a rustling of cloth comes from the hand which disappears in front of the body click click as the brush is dipped the latest line draws a frontier between what is and what is not yet the future shrinks line by line with unperturbable regularity without accident time knows no accident either from outside or in the movement of its perpetual arrival anyway time doesn't have an outside but there is this passion of the painter's his passionate attention to the inexorable process that is life which nothing ever hurries it just seems to on occasion the hand is no longer at exactly the same height in relation to the face that's the only change the only accident but that accident is not accidental it's part of the movement that controls the relationship what is it that is being inscribed here numbers of course and something else wondering what else Opalka's last words come back to mind they explain nothing but they are a guide while another line is finished and a new one immediately begun the hand disappears click click scratching back of neck a sigh steps back moves forward to examine the picture I'm just thinking says Opalka turning round that if nature gives me the good fortune to reach complete whiteness and seven sevens the emotion will be so great that I'll drop dead on the spot and when I project myself forwards to that moment I can imagine how you can kill yourself out of emotion I do this projecting a lot while carrying on with what I'm doing I move around in the past and the future I have a sensation of being in the present and when it throws me into the future it's a drug that makes me levitate he turns back to the picture then away again which again goes to show that a *detail* is not a picture but an opportunity to move through time and create emotion he faces the picture raises his hand mutters there are lots of things going on in the mind of a man who does this what number three million eight hundred and three thousand four hundred and fifty life he says manifests itself so strongly and what I do is so adequate to its manifestation that the imagination can go off in all directions doing what I do is so easy that while I'm doing it I can go off in all directions levitating here there and everywhere and I use the word deliberately Yves Klein used to try to levitate but it wasn't real you either fling yourself out of the window or you don't we need to find other ways of flying through the mind

23 April 1985/2

you can't impose a truth on people it has to grow with experience it changes the whole time with me it's the opposite mine goes on confirming itself how can you prove the truth except by logic what I call truth derives from the structure of my concept which produces something that you can't help but agree with it's fascinating that such a thing is possible it's a truth in the same way that an irreplaceable word in a sentence is true all my *details* are bricks in a single picture whose parts are scattered in New York Paris Tokyo Berlin etc. there are *details* everywhere not just anywhere I'm going to have a retrospective in New York a little retrospective has been in my plans for the last twenty years straight after the opening in New York I have to go to Munich because I'm a member of the organising committee of an event in aid of Solidarnosc the artists invited have agreed to create a work on the spot and they'll all be sold for the benefit of Solidarnosc I need to have finished this *detail* before I move on to the *travel cards* I'll be giving to Solidarnosc I invented *travel cards* to block off an escape route journeys might be an opportunity to do nothing but now I can use them to pursue my concept through these *cards* and the last one has to be finished before I get back here and start a new *detail* the process must not be interrupted painters decide when their picture is finished it's not me who'll decide but life Malevich must have thought he'd attained the truth with his white on white square and Pollock too and Monet with his water-lilies if nature has managed to make things like that by chance Pollock said to himself then I can do the same what others achieve through chaos I set out to do through logic I was delighted to be exhibited next to Pollock because I'm the opposite of him with me truth is entirely determined I have given birth to a system which develops so that everything is constantly changing while remaining constantly the same Prigogine would say I recognise that there is some truth in that but is that all Opalka replies no that isn't all but if you want more I can't help you I am trying to get close to something that is one hundred percent the way I foresee it to be the aim is to express the truth of our limitations it's also a kind of diary without fantasies or snapshots expressing the energy of my life yes the painted trace of my life is made out of my energy I am in the process of creating the knowledge of what I do in that sense I am like an unskilled worker acquiring a skill we are bombarded with too many images I suspect we are going to become empty of images my approach attempts to rescue an image by means of a non-image there is too much image and picture pollution an artist who lives for fifty years can now pollute half the world with his output what's the point of so many pictures I'm only making one I began in the spirit of a painter because I was one then I wanted to do more than paint and certainly not less Opalka is sitting on the floor on a large fur covered cushion more or less in the centre of his studio the wooden entrance door seems hidden away in a deep recess in the thick wall right in the corner of the room there is just one double window with fourteen panes in each side all the walls are of bare masonry impeccably pointed the one opposite the entrance has a fireplace in the middle with a lintel made out of one long stone with a moulding along the top the floor is covered in gray and white carpet which looks the same light ochre colour as the walls along the wall by the door are arranged a glass fronted cabinet four shelves with papers and books on two small suitcases on the floor in front of the furniture papers spread about an orange shirt a white push-button telephone a unit with nine drawers two others with six trays a stereo system two pictures propped up against each other along the end wall a speaker with a very thick book in an old binding on top a microphone on a stand a white curtain hanging in folds in front of which stands the easel carrying the *detail* in progress another microphone on a stand another speaker then along the fireplace wall some wires connected to a small flat device a pile of frames for *travel cards* the first unwrapped the others packed two by two in five packets of bubble plastic then after the fireplace a wooden bench behind which stand five prepared canvasses then along the window wall on either side of the window five *travel cards* set out in a row a spotlamp pointing at an old dark brown wooden table with two folding leaves supported by plain legs and one carved one on the table books catalogues a box of tissues next to it a high backed wooden chair on the floor around it piles of catalogues art magazines books in the middle of the room the large cushion with Opalka sitting on it and a folded blanket then in front of the current *detail* a large four track TEAC tape recorder with it a copier and the spotlamp illuminating the work and the metal stand carrying the umbrella reflector and a camera I take a photo of myself every evening when it's dark so that the light is always the same to start with I didn't pay any attention to my shirt and I noticed that instead of capturing the ageing process I had only recorded different sorts of shirts so now I always keep the same one there behind the easel Opalka stands up opens the window closes the wooden shutters to keep out the light stands in front of his picture takes off his jacket and shirt grabs the one hanging behind the easel puts it on come and look he says see next to the camera I have a mirror so I can see myself the reflectasol makes sure that the background lighting is always the same he points out the mirror and the cable release hanging down from the camera stand over here with your shoulders close to the canvas that's right gently squeeze the cable release having done so I withdraw and Opalka takes up the same position sets off the flash removes his shirt puts the daytime one back on again and goes to open the shutters

24 April 1985

Opalka switches on the spotlamp picks up the pot and brush stands in front of the *detail* and begins to paint oh he says my glasses he comes and picks them up off the table I still haven't got used to working with glasses on I've only had them for two or three pictures the trembling leaves of a lime tree sweep across the window from my chair the spotlamp hides the head and the hand jeans thick white shirt sleeveless waistcoat shimmering in the light the left shoulder is held back blocking out the right towards the far end of the current line the left hand appears in profile wrapped around the pot it is quarter to two in the afternoon I need to get myself a big desk says Opalka coming away from his canvas towards me then I could look out of the window when I'm writing he returns to the picture the light shines through the right hand side of his hair the brush hand emerges from the head its shadow falls vertically on the face parallel to the angle made by the bent forefinger the telephone rings Opalka turns round groans bends down hello yes I remember yes I know what it's about fine thank you he puts the phone down straightens up that's kind he says getting back to work half hidden by the reflector whose lower edge makes a white line across his shoulders sigh shift to the left a new line begins the brush handle moves slowly the hand advances by little leaps which make a rubbing sound I have time to count to eleven between two rubbing noises then to nine then to seven then to nine one time in two it coincides with the brush's trip towards the pot then it's the waistcoat that makes a rubbing noise where are you up to three million eight hundred and three thousand there he says moving to his left I break the number and the three starts the next line followed by five hundred and sixty eight I sit down on the ground next to a fat catalogue called *Art and Time* on page 236 of which is written While Opalka and Darboven attempt to preserve lived time by means of continuously repeated letters or numbers are you attempting I say to preserve lived time that expostulates Opalka is nonsense we are so full of words that people repeat with no thought for their meaning he has merely turned his head which is now in profile against the surface the current line emerges from his lips as he returns to the picture he extends it a sentence from Thomas Bernhardt's *The Lime Works* that I had read that morning passes through my mind reality is in reality always different always the opposite in reality it is truly reality all the fingers of the right hand are tucked in except the thumb the tip of which makes little movements like a mouth chewing the hand swivels gently on the wrist drawing tiny circles end of the line three million eight hundred and three thousand seven hundred and thirteen Opalka announces and stops goes over to the fireplace washes his brush there are little bits stuck to the canvas he says

I get them off with a razor blade he picks up a razor blade from the edge of the fireplace and does to the picture what he has just said then putting down the blade he picks up brush and pot again the last line seems straight as long as I concentrate on the direction and not the thickness which varies with different shades of white the hand is preceded now by its shadow preceded in its turn by the shadow of the hair the hand like the line is on a level with the neck the picture rises up to the ceiling and its top disappears behind a beam the current line and the one before are whiter and shinier than the previous five or six above them there are no more lines but a number of circular zones in which yes the eye sees what might be a street plan now that the end of the line is approaching it seems to follow the chin three million eight hundred and three thousand eight hundred and twelve but I'm going to put the twelve here announces Opalka returning to the side where the numbers start the eye moves slowly back up the picture in fact the last five or six lines are about as white and transparent as each other then the lines above don't look like lines at all but more like contours on a map the right hand advances I can make out only the tip of the thumb and the first two knuckles of the index and middle fingers the rest is so tightly tucked under that the hand seems mutilated three million eight hundred and three thousand one hundred and fifty eight the eight is nice and clear he says coming to wash his brush in the glass perched on the edge of the mantelpiece I wash it a lot because acrylic dries very quickly and that can spoil the brush the new line runs just beneath the curve of the chin the shadow of the elbow moves across the bar of the easel on which the *detail* rests rubbing sounds I count to eight then nine then seven click click seven again the thumb bends straightens bends during the clicking as the brush is dipped the knees bend and the parquet creaks beneath the wooden clogs three million eight hundred and three thousand nine hundred and five and this time it falls nicely at the end of the line back to the beginning head bowed hand concealed to start with then rising to the east of the chin brush cleaned by the fireplace this time the notch made by the current line is very clear showing up as a furrow a tiny slit through which the eye can pass and move around between the figures only to lose its way almost at once then the gaze rises back to the figured surface discovers the light cascading among the curves in swirling splashes sounds of rubbing cloth the height of the current line in relation to body positions depends of course on where the observer is the line runs at the moment below the chin the figures are inscribed in a motion that has the fluidity of writing what sort of thickness are your lines four or five millimetres he says but it depends a lot on how tired I am the numbers are bigger in the evening smaller in the morning he leaves the picture goes to clean his brush leaves it on the edge of the mantelpiece along with the pot opens the cabinet moves some papers around the tape measure he says going over to the table he searches opens a drawer takes off his glasses goes back to the cabinet searches in the bottom I must have left it somewhere during the repairs he looks again on the table opens a briefcase shuts it I can't find it I'm not going to look downstairs it's somewhere around I don't know where he takes up his brush once more stirs the pot while walking back to the *detail* bends down to the line there are various zones up and down the figured surface bands of different widths which perhaps correspond to different days but they blur together in the centre where the light is they can only be made out for a second round the edges the numbers are little white tags they fit together like roof tiles but without any regularity or rather in a contradiction constantly repeated all over the canvas with an irregular regularity a given detail seems regular and the whole irregular hence the impression of space rather than surface swirling space three million eight hundred and four thousand and forty eight brush washing with a great clatter against the glass like beating eggs each line is made out of visual sequences each sequence corresponds to the amount of paint the brush takes up and exhausts before returning to the pot sequences do not correspond to numbers or to a regular exhaustion of paint fading out in a similar way every time here and there you find a short run of figures in dense white which don't necessarily coincide with a number they punctuate the surface it may be that their dispersal across the surface destroys its linearity which would make their frequency a matter of aesthetics if only that could be proven but it's impossible it's as if these white bits were leaps of white across the surface qualitative leaps one day the length of a number will no doubt correspond to the exhaustion of a brush load but that length increases infinitely slowly reaching one million only added one extra figure ten million will add only one more it took twenty years to get from one to three million eight hundred thousand so it will take more than thirty years to go from that three million eight hundred thousand to ten million and from ten to a hundred million would take four hundred and fifty years of work at over eight hours per day the parquet floor creaks the body is leaning forwards the right hand writes the left is tucked in to the waist elbow bent how many numbers with each brush load between two and three but sometimes only one and each number contains seven figures they're very much alive to start with I wondered whether I should make each figure of equal intensity of white particularly as the differences were very visible against a black background logic provided the answer why not let the white run out and keep the trace of a sort of movement something like footprints of course stupid people think it's done deliberately to look nice if there is an aesthetic effect it's in the Platonic sense and not to look nice looking nice is pejorative my determination is not about pleasing people that's all a lot of painting is about he goes to wash the brush beating it against the sides of the glass then comes back to the picture and begins a new line catalogue of an exhibition in Essen in 1973 a photo showing five *details* in perspective the first nearest the lens is a visual explosion with black holes some of the numbers are strikingly in relief the curves made up of overlapping staircases whose steps sometimes seems to be advancing sometimes regressing with a magnifying glass and in order to work out where the *detail* comes I decipher three hundred and seventy three thousand zero zero four visual and temporal matter are for a moment identical as far as the eye can see to the ends of time raising my head I can see through the window the sun's disk with clouds sliding across it above a scrawny cypress turned brown by the frost three million eight hundred and four thousand two hundred and ninety nine on the previous double page spread in the catalogue twelve *details* three on one wall nine on the one adjoining it at right angles through the magnifying glass their surface is like tweed on the previous page close up of a *detail* I notice of course the change from six nines to one followed by six noughts in the early *details* he says the quantity of numbers was greater I wondered about legibility I only dip the brush in the paint when I start a number I don't care whether the end is legible then I occasionally dip the brush before it runs out for a moment the body at work is almost completely in profile the left leg thrust backwards makes an acute angle with the shoulders the right hand emerges from the right shoulder making another acute angle with the surface of the canvas three million eight hundred and four thousand three hundred and thirty seven the newly begun line extends out from the edge of the hair on the back of the neck exhibition from the sixth of November to the second of December nineteen seventy three the first monograph was written by Bozena Kowalska it came out in Polish in Cracow in nineteen seventy six the preface is reprinted in German English and French in the front of the faces collection published by Ottenhausen Verlag in Munich in an edition of six hundred it contains a selection of daily photos taken during the period between two million and three and a record every *detail* is accompanied by a recording on magnetic tape of my voice speaking the numbers while I paint them and a picture of my face three million eight hundred and four thousand four hundred and thirty three are there any traces that could be said to be linked to the specific moment yes he says there are differences of inner or bodily vibration silence right I'm going to take the photo he puts down the pot washes the brush yes there are several factors which make a difference first the humidity because paint reacts to the humidity of the air and then it's impossible to get exactly the same proportion of water in the mixture to the nearest drop Opalka takes off his jacket and throws it on the ground against the tape machine takes off his shirt and throws it on top of the jacket grabs the one behind the easel puts it on while walking over to the window closes the heavy wooden shutters returns to the picture poses while holding the cable release in his left hand click flash Opalka makes a note of the number reached when the photo was taken three million eight hundred and four thousand four hundred and forty four there are four fours together he says putting the photographic shirt back behind the easel he picks up his clothes opens the shutters finishes dressing in front of the fireplace picks up his glasses his pot his brush and goes to carry on the line click click long sigh by the way he says facing the canvas I must also point out the vibration of the nerves which leaves its mark the right hand writes close up to the shoulder three million eight hundred and four thousand four hundred and eighty two new line beginning beneath the right ear and staying there for twenty centimetres or so the hand is a small animal ferreting about coming back with the tip of the brush drawing each figure rather than writing it but how to describe the difference each figure is made up of fragments of lines the zero for instance is two semicircles the four a slanting line and two bars the eight two circles I was once asked to draw a number specially on my picture it was a torture to me but they were so insistent I gave in when I'd drawn the first figure it looked so awful I shouted stop just one figure and it was all wrong I rubbed it out straight away because acrylic doesn't dry immediately Opalka walks away from the *detail* to wash his brush then returns it's not possible he says to copy a *detail* not even for me because the rhythm changes what I painted two or three years ago is quite different it's like the ageing process he goes to put down brush and pot sits down on the large cushion the material that you see in a *detail* is made from a certain quantity of energy there's no faking that the background of the first *detail* was black and as the devil of painting was still strong within me I chose a red background with carmine figures for the second one I wanted to play around with the aggressive contrast afterwards I tried black on red before taking the decision to use gray which contains all the other colours and which I kept stable until 1972 it's not so different from the first black background which looks gray against the white figures especially since tempera forces you to make the figures quite large so the black on the first *detail* was pretty well covered only the first was done in tempera and the red one too then I changed to acrylic I worked on the first *detail* for seven months the next two took me just into sixty-seven the stable gray lasted about five years at the end of which time I knew my decision was irrevocable I don't know how long it will take me to get to pure white and then how long I'll carry on with the white itself of course but I say white on white can theoretically last for ever yes he says but not in practice because the difficulty and the fatigue will probably mean that I don't paint more than one a year I've never been able to stand in front of my canvasses without feeling emotion whereas people would think they were cold and empty they surprise me every time with their power how far away are you I say from pure white I can't estimate he says with any certainty you know I prepare between ten and twenty canvasses at a time to avoid contamination of the brushes or mixture but a drop of water can affect things as well as the atmospheric humidity each series I prepare approaches the desired one percent with a small margin for error then again no matter how perfectly I realise my concept my old canvasses become darker with age or through air pollution as in Turin in the end it makes no difference to my programme because the changes brought about by time can also be reduced by time my canvasses are fragile they may be damaged or stained sixteen of them have been round twenty galleries we decided to call a halt incidentally that's a big problem today too many exhibitions a mad rush to move pictures about here there and everywhere I love Morandi a wise and lucid man with a certain existential melancholy that's what you think when you stand in front of a Morandi but when there are a hundred of them you lose a lot of it with my *details* I don't run that risk that's what makes me new and different quantity illuminates the idea instead of compromising it

30 April 1990

for the extremist i.e. demanding painter that I am it is no longer possible to make pictures after Malevich Pollock Rothko Klein I created an opportunity for myself using the space-time offered by my life I belong to a generation which has understood that you have to express one thing just one you can't play with limits when it is obvious from the start that you won't be able to extend them imagine Pollock or Klein becoming hyper-realists Klein was contemplating it he would have nullified all his thinking erased his achievement like a god going back to walking instead of levitating what I have embarked upon I will continue right through my life without cheating either myself or the public it would be impossible to put a single square centimetre of my work somewhere else you are free of the problem of quality because it's irrelevant you need to discover the truth of your situation then stick to it a bit like always looking out of the same window if you want to have time to deepen the way you see you have to concentrate on just a single object otherwise you start imagining things and run the risk of it all going wrong I'm not saying that my answer is the only one I realised some time around 1960 that the explosion of the visual arts in the twentieth century meant that progress was no longer possible we have reached the limit we are in the silence that follows the explosion that silence is what I paint and it's going to last for a long time artists like Johns or Warhol aren't part of this silence theirs is the art of pleasing the crowd they have nothing to do with what seems to me important in art which is to create a space for man to take refuge in Warhol was able to laugh at himself and other people he was an idol and that's just not serious I speak not as a reactionary but an extremist I'm very demanding on the subject of truth i.e. logic and coherence to start with if I left out a figure from my process I would go back to it go back to underline my weakness I wanted to bear witness to that moral aspect I realised that a mistake proves the logic of the system it's not a mistake but a weakness it's not a matter of achieving perfection but of recognising the limitations of our work and the honest thing to say is I fill my life with an almost insane activity because what I do forces me to work enormously hard the work of an active nihilist in order to make something with no conceivable use not even in the humanistic sense the confusion of the 80s with the trans-avant-garde and the new figuration lets us see the 60s and 70s in their real perspective it was an extraordinary period the most important thing in the twentieth century is conceptual art Johns Stella Warhol were worthwhile artists at first but they threw themselves into their own decadence I am not someone who can see a solution but I don't want to waste my time rousing crowds to instant euphoria art today is dominated by the media and the present is all that counts but any work that is going to last compromises the present Warhol is an illustrator not someone in the line going back to Lascaux he has no worthy relationship with that great past there was no banality at Altamira banality was Warhol's reality but in the most vulgar sense Buren in comparison shows a great deal of intelligence and ability to adapt to whatever is going on around him we are similar except that I am always doing the same thing and it's always different like life it's no accident that I use my name as a title OPALKA 1965 is the date when the concept was born the date when this constantly changing thing began to move every time I add a number I change the whole thing just as every minute changes us I paint my canvasses with number zero brushes which is illogical on the part of the manufacturer since zero doesn't exist it's an absence if I talk about zero and one it's a way of saying I am still part of the same thing Buren is close to me in time but the difference between me and him and others like him is that I am always doing the same thing without it ever being finished whereas they always present an object complete in its formal proposition and definition but which lacks the dynamic property of being one single and unique thing like life Buren does a staircase in São Paulo then some chairs in Venice then some sails in Berlin then some columns in Paris it's all very intelligent and dialectical and social and contemporary whereas I could just as well be born in some future universe or be a Greek from the age of Pythagoras a Greek busy constructing an ethical and moral and logical image representing a raison d'être a reason not to go mad or give in to despair what point of reference can there be for a man in our universe if not some balance between the two poles of morality and logic the visual universe which is mine went through its explosion and from that I drew the strength to go as far as I have an Opalkos would not have been able to do that and could therefore never have existed I am close to the minimalists and conceptualists but my way of working is at odds with the conceptual world whose child I am in post-56 Poland after the Polish October people knew about the avant-garde and were able to work in comparable freedom to countries in the West except that there was no market the society in which I was living had no interest in my moral and logical approach neither did the State I could express whatever I was thinking it's true I was quite free to do it but without any support from galleries or institutions so why bother simply because I could tell myself that at least I was doing what I thought was right as for how to make a living there was engraving which gave me the means of physical existence my good fortune is that the world I was living in left me with no illusions I could see life's limitations more clearly than elsewhere in a planned economy a man perceives his project and his end with much greater clarity than in western society in that sense I was in a privileged position for there was no way for me to extol my revolution like Yves Klein at the Sorbonne revolution a word full of hope but also of illusions when people compare me to Buren Toroni Darboven Kawara they are quite wrong on the level of the raison d'être of what I do they misunderstand because they see only the superficial similarity dots dabs stripes seem like an aesthetic game rather than a logical necessity you can use more stripes or dabs or fewer there's no reason to fix their movement to stop it everything depends on an arbitrary decision there is a deep misunderstanding a conceptual misunderstanding at the heart of our movement if Buren Toroni or I have decided to do the same thing all the time that's because it's a dramatic thing to do but it's also a trap like adding water to water all the Burens and Toronis and Kawaras are products of the artist's arbitrary decisions they look all right in an exhibition the idea works well enough but what a sad result if you're going to commit suicide you should do it with an image that gives dignity to man suicide is banal it's not a drama I must create a strength with my despair I want my suicide to have a meaning looking at Toroni Buren there's no question of suicide they're aesthetes not artists aware that you can't do it any more the great difference between those guys and me is that I'm a happy pessimist I haven't given up I knew it was no longer possible to paint and I've created the last picture worthy of the culture of our past humanity created a miracle which is the picture Johns and the others have betrayed that divine inspiration I'm talking about the drama of no longer being able to create icons after Mondrian Malevich Pollock he was a really desperate man was Pollock and well aware of the drama of the picture his pictures are all movement they're chaotic whereas in mine everything is organised chaos is made into intelligence from Altamira to the names I've just mentioned via the Mona Lisa you see the same demanding intelligence my extremism comes from those extraordinary pictures and the realisation that nobody is doing anything like that any more I wanted to rescue the dignity of intelligence I'm talking about the drama of the picture after thousands of years in the course of which we created the still image moving images are a joke like a tart who wiggles her bum too much which reminds me of a joke the client says to the tart keep still I'm the one who's paying life is short so people go for cheap effects I hate that I hate art that plays games that's why I'm so against Warhol all that has nothing to do with what I call art of course it is based initially on intelligence the artist isn't a gorilla but he has to be passionate first and foremost that's more important than intelligence extraordinary things happened in the art of the 70s but there was a misunderstanding too often we used our intelligence to have fun with but what to say and how to say it is an emotion more powerful than intelligence the Bible puts the Word at the origin of everything but I think emotion is the origin to create anything you need emotion of course you mustn't fall into the trap of dualism intelligence led me forward and enlightened me but it was always inseparable from emotion my project and so my destiny are down to intelligence humanity has to pay a much higher price than people think to make something more noble than present reality I've no desire to make enemies but I do have a duty to point out differences everything in my work obeys a necessity but with an emotional and moral side to it the others are just playing what they do is reversible they can go back and correct it but you can't correct life I can never erase anything I do I am committed to it in the same way as you commit yourself to accepting life I am not like Bob Ryman buying up his earlier pictures to destroy them because he doesn't think they're up to his present standards Ryman is a major artist a true professional who has had the strength to create himself he belongs to the family of the last true painters except that he's wedded to the picture as form and aesthetic object a position I can appreciate but which doesn't interest me in the slightest I have some regard for the formal qualities of his aesthetic solutions but I find the drama of the picture as object quite inadequate now what is important to me is the drama of man seen through the picture of man incorporated into it for me painting in itself could never be a reason to carry on that's why I've taken the liberty of comparing myself to an Ancient Greek seeking the foundation of moral answers the Greek materialists are more significant than any founders of religions anything founded on faith is less important than what is founded on reason I am attempting to base myself on behavioural logic trying not to be arbitrary and to find rational answers it's almost a non-starter because humanity is much more irrational than I ever imagined I often say there's a big difference between knowing and understanding our world knows many things but does it understand them L'arte e facile it is if you understand it Chiari himself didn't understand what he was saying art doesn't rescue the person but the message it was crucial for me that what my art was saying should remain coherent with what was happening in the profession there I was in my studio thinking to myself it's impossible to make pictures nowadays there was not much that aroused emotion in me to what could I devote my life in a dignified way like everybody in the avant-garde I wanted to invent something new the glorification of novelty makes people rush into the next trend Marcel Duchamp was both very intelligent and very destructive he had answers which tended towards a total impasse but in his drive to demystify art he opened up all the doors but inside each one he put down his own mark which prevented people from exploiting them yet his intelligence couldn't stop the trends and they prevented him from inventing things which could have safeguarded our dignity Klein was saved by death Duchamp played chess Duchamp gave us proof of his intelligence and courage but did he create true works of art i.e. things which move us and are not simply a source of pleasure for the intelligence looking at Yves Klein's monochromes I see intelligence but I also feel incredible emotion at the São Paulo biennial festival there was a Duchamp retrospective with all his objects but you can learn just as much about them from a book I don't get the same emotion from a reproduction that I get from a Malevich or a Klein Duchamp didn't create objects of fascination except to the intelligence his inventions turn out to be jokes which work all right but don't get you very far the difference between Klein and me is that I prove my love while he is content just to talk about it he enjoyed finding brilliant spectacular answers a glorification of the intelligence rather than of the work still I consider him the most astonishing artist of the twentieth century Malevich ended in shame with the excuse of political pressure yet an uncompromising attitude to the message you want to get across always gives you a chance of doing something worthwhile the Marxist aesthetic theorists were often right in what they were saying but the more timid hangers-on imagined that the most simplistic approach would be the most profitable if they had opted for difficulty and quality the authorities might have taken them as a reference Malevich didn't have to sink so low even in the most unpleasant of situations and with restricted freedom you can make quality stand out by being determined and uncompromising compromise empties the work of its substance intelligence is not enough it takes strength as well I'm thinking of Beuys I had a lot of respect for him as an artist he was morally very committed but also stuffed full of illusions he was fortunate enough to be able to create in a typically German mood of euphoria a sort of obsession his naiveté sometimes scared me for instance his slogan I love America America loves me is stiflingly pretentious and lacking in perspective it scared me because it was based on irrationality when you get morality without logic you never know where you are but his excitement had a certain quality a strength about it intelligence isn't enough you also need that strength and he obviously had it he was a kind of sorcerer who created powerful situations it was a power I could never understand when the German pacifists scream for Peace I am in favour of peace but it scares me something built up around Beuys that turned him into the Führer of contemporary art the crowds of little people in the art world were blinded by the phenomenon Beuys's messianic attitude made me uncomfortable like all those of my generation who have been injured in a certain way by Germany with his felt hat his sledge and coyotes Beuys was able to translate his experience in a way that showed inventive intelligence and a mixture of spirituality and physical strength people worshipped the sorcerer who created amazing things and they were truly amazing and forgot where they came from their German source more real than their tartar source once he had an audience Beuys became even more inventive he was carried along levitated by them but when the audience goes away the works are in danger of losing all their substance nowadays how can you create a situation in which to die with dignity we need to accept physical death and not brood on it as the Christians did brooding on a corpse is hell perhaps a dead person imagines different situations from a living one like a dream that can never be told to anyone god is an extraordinary idea we invented to establish a scale of the most implausible qualities and to give us some space because our space is limited by time and by population man can only exist together with nature and he's probably going to come unstuck with his cosmic expansion the limits remain even when they've been pushed back a little it's a pessimistic but inspiring thought our smallness means we must look for points of reference on our own scale it's possible to be small and dignified sooner or later there'll be a catastrophe we can still solve some of the problems but man's responsibility is not limited to a few generations we need to think in millennia quantity is going to reduce quality every change contains a trap quantity is always a trap optimistic thinking must always be based on the most pessimistic forecasts if we're going to save the human race we need to dramatise the situation lucidity requires a negative but moral discourse the ecologists are not lucid enough they are propounding an unthinkable future the pessimists are the ones who are most committed to positive solutions for the future it's not true that we could feed everybody not true that we could put up mirrors everywhere to provide heat suppose it were true what happens you put up more and more fill the place up no what you need to do is rescue the human qualities barbarism will always resurface in the face of danger or privation mankind hasn't changed can't change here I am doing a strip-tease thinking about the world for I have always been moved by that thought since I started to travel in the West I find too much euphoria in Poland I refused to choose between the Party and the Church between ideology and religious despair if the Poles are now on their knees economically it's perhaps because they're on their knees in the churches I have no illusions about mankind people forget that war is still conceivable when everybody has a pistol it reduces aggression if it hadn't been for the bomb Europe would already have had several wars the human race is capable of being German it all depends on the context that's why I prefer the Germans including Beuys to avoid that context one day in Munich a German friend tells me we too should be allowed to make plans for humanity I didn't say anything to avoid screwing up the whole evening but I thought to myself you have loads of technological answers but as for humanism even if you do have some good ideas we need to be very careful the thought of Socrates hasn't been misused because he was a pessimist but as for Marx the future of the world really worries me which is why morally and logically I feel committed to going on with what I am doing even if I find out that today is the end of the world that sort of emotion makes me different from a Zen Buddhist monk who wants to lose the feeling of his relationship to humanity I paint and listen to the news I have my little black and white television here because I can't stand colour in my place of work I love life otherwise what would be the point of worrying about humanity if it had no joie de vivre life is beautiful isn't it it's not the idea of dying that makes me sad but the idea that life's meaning and dignity could die what I am doing is painting the portrait of a life when I finish a *detail* or a *travel card* I'm afraid of exploding of dying because for that moment I am outside i.e. outside my home outside my skin until I've started something new I'm not there as soon as the first number has been drawn I feel better even if it still isn't enough it takes a whole line before I am back inside myself after a quarter of a century I have built up something beyond my control it's very physical very organic a visualisation of an active life if my work is absurd it's the absurdity of existence a manual worker regards absurd work as the shameful part of a world which forces people into slavery in order to eat I am someone who has made a choice and wants to keep his dignity the unfair thing is that I have had time to understand whereas my father didn't a large part of mankind works without having time to think and as soon as it manages to free up a bit of time it gets filled with stupid things and gadgets we only live to be able to ask interesting questions but for that moment when I've finished one and not yet started the next I am not in my body I could drop down dead it's quite dramatic because a self-destructive force builds up in me a dynamic that creates so much tension I could burst the anxiety is all the greater because I'm no longer sustained by the strength which derives from what I'm doing and because once I've been interrupted I run the risk pardon me for saying so of depriving art history of a non-arbitrary end I believe in unity dualistic thinking is in my view naive you can't separate good from evil it's no accident that I began with black and plan to end up with white the whole journey from one to the other being the image of an existence called Opalka the vitality of this image is ultimately greater than my own what I'm doing is what everybody does except that I'm doing it as an image of everybody my work seems egocentric but it's really universal because it makes accumulated activity visible if you could see all the coal my father dug out that would be his œuvre I've deliberately made my own into the image of a lifetime's activity a life lived in full awareness of my solidarity with the world of work I'm making something absurd but which poses vital questions for everyone's existence my approach allows me to do something which is good for nothing other than to rescue meaning it's like sitting down on the ground to look at the sky it's about working to have enough time to look at infinity in the sky Opalka is sitting on the large fur covered cushion he went there as soon as we came into the studio he told me there was a problem with the *detail* he's about to start and I thought that he would begin work straight away to repair the surface damaged by contact with other canvasses during the preparation process but no he started talking making my hand rush across the pages of my notebook the great picture in waiting there in the spotlight looking whiter and whiter as the day darkens Opalka turns to look at it it's a mirror in which you can see infinity mirrors have no colour it's us who give them their colour he gets up and goes over to the picture climbs on a bench to examine the surface at the top I put several layers on to get this gray background six seven sometimes eight or nine to get the surface just right for the brush to draw the figures without scratching looking up from the floor I see the metal stand with the camera rear-view mirror and reflector on it Opalka gets down walks over to the fireplace shakes a plastic bottle tips out its contents arms himself with various tools climbs back on the bench paints the top left corner paints the edge with a little brush whose presence I guess rather than see is it the same one he uses for the figures no it's a different one I use a new brush on every picture for the figures I get it out all fresh and new when I'm on the point of starting jeans white shirt the light sparkles in the white hair Opalka gets down off the bench in his left hand he holds a little black pot perhaps a film container into which he has poured his paint he kneels down and begins restoration work on the bottom the retouched patches are tiny scarcely more than a few square centimetres along the edge couldn't they wait until later yes but it wouldn't help me to get started any quicker as I have to wait for the top to dry left knee on the ground whole body leaning forwards tiny dabbings of the brush along the edge of the canvas Opalka climbs back on the bench examines the surface right shoulder forwards the first line is possible I can repair the rest as I go the background is intact for the first line he gets down goes over to the glass fronted cabinet gets out a blue cardboard box takes from it a new brush it's the famous number zero brush he says as he walks over to the fireplace where he shakes the white plastic bottle once more he tips some into the pot stirs with the brush then right in the top left corner of the picture the hand does thumb loosening exercises I'm starting with a four four million four hundred and eighty five thousand six hundred and eighteen flexing of the thumb now it's the arm loosening up as far as the shoulder chin in profile hand moving forwards a little every three or four seconds slight creaking also the noise of clogs on bench which calls attention to the red socks the sleeve is rolled up a little and hangs in a loop below the wrist the epaulette on the right shoulder is rucked up the body above the waist is at a slant the elbow moves the line appears above the left shoulder damp as it advances a slight white dampness along the very top edge thumb index and middle finger are all that can be seen of the right hand the thumb joint moves whereas the fingers are locked together the elbow sways up and down while the mass of the hand advances topped by its shadow which moves more than it does the moving of writing I say to myself wondering immediately what that means I have the impression of an organ performing some vital and mysterious function the right edge is getting close the back is tense attentive vigilant sigh the shadow falls outside the surface that's it I'm not going to do any more I can't I'll stop here the head bends the arm turns round I'm stopping here because I can't transfer across to the other side because the background isn't ready is the last number complete yes of course four million four hundred and eighty five thousand six hundred and sixty one the line isn't finished its white dampness glistens in the light if you cut a number in two it bleeds the logic runs out of it rather than the meaning I get a great deal of pleasure from what I do but it's very tiring incredible pleasure to either side of the *detail* resting on its adjustable easel there is a microphone on a stand just as there always used to be the one on the right pointing right the one on the left pointing left and two speakers Opalka has taken his shoes off he scrutinises the vertical edges and retouches them here and there the wall of bare stones is beige in the light it's impossible to correct the drawing of the figures says Opalka it would be like trying to go back to yesterday you can't ever redo a *detail* because it's a period of lived not measured time for the same reason you can't make a fake the beginning and the end are all of a piece like our skin he leaves the picture and comes over he stands with his back to the picture the important thing is what I call mental whiteness first unlike all monochrome whites it isn't blinding that's because the others are all physical whereas mine is mental it's the glorification of a white which is a whole life working towards the light physically all whites are white but they aren't comparable to an emotional and mental white which isn't some easy answer a conceptual short cut but a sort of stations of the cross towards whiteness I'm not after a colour but a substance of white that's all and if the canvas is stained or damaged it still carries the message despite the violence it has undergone a church does not need to be new to fulfil its function at the top of the *detail* a narrow white border catches the light a little more than the rest of the surface Opalka takes a blank sheet of paper and draws a rectangle that he says pointing to the page is the whole picture and that he says showing the upper right and lower left corners of the rectangle is the *detail* he draws two other rectangles this line is eternity he says extending the left hand side of the first rectangle upwards it comes from there in the first *detail* and it's the figure one then it continues like this he says joining the lower right corner of the first rectangle to the upper left of the second then the lower right of the second to the upper left of the third

1 May 1990

standing in the light the hand high up I'm sorry but I'm going to have to stop because the paint is too runny he leaves the picture turns his back on it the paint must be neither too runny nor too thick I have to navigate between the two extremes it's impossible to fix the balance once and for all just like life he goes over to the fireplace adds a drop of paint to the pot stirs it in returns to the picture the second line has been started he has just drawn two numbers to make the jump the first line contains some gleaming segments and others so pale that it is hard to make them out jeans white shirt red socks clogs as yesterday with the addition of a waistcoat the back of which shimmers in the light the thumb joint twitches the wrist presses against the canvas the elbow moves and the shoulder too as a twitch runs along the arm and is absorbed by the body I leave the middle of the room and go and sit by the left hand corner of the fireplace I can see the right ear and the corner of the glasses the head is pointing towards the hand the cheek quivers the arm drops when it is time to dip the brush in the pot the head follows slumping down the hand goes back into position the thumbnail glints the second line is half done the shadow of the brush rules a line through the hollow between thumb and forefinger whereas the shadow of the hand against the canvas is a plume of feathers emerging from the wrist from behind like this the whole body looks like a holder for the hand four million four hundred and eighty five thousand seven hundred and nine the line ends on this complete number Opalka moves to the left stops looks at the canvas the right shoulder dips then as if on a balancing arm the left brings it back up again the hand goes down the brush is dipped click click the hand goes back into position I count to thirteen before activity on the same spot ends in a move here's an interesting thing he says I've got to seven hundred and eighteen but I began on six hundred and eighteen so I've done fifty numbers to the line which means my figures are neither too big nor too small it's like a rev counter for an engine some people thought that as my pictures got more expensive I'd make the figures bigger in principle I have aimed to keep the same size from the beginning but it does vary the nought for instance takes up more room than the one the third line is now some thirty centimetres long beneath the right ear a sinew stands out on the tensed neck the chins points slightly upwards the extremity of the forearm emerges from a ruff of shirt the hand seems to be pecking in its on the spot activity from time to time the corner of the mouth wrinkles the profile is tense attentive a nervous tremor runs through it now and then it is this that lifts the corner of the mouth when the arm goes down to dip the brush the face describes a circle opposite the canvas as if it were revolving around the hub of the gaze riveted to the line in progress the body's shadow on the canvas is very dark up to the waist then it vaporises into the light the painting action runs from the elbow to the wrist hardly moving the hand at all the out of sight arm the one holding the pot makes a phallus-like shadow four million four hundred and eighty five thousand and I'm starting the line with seven hundred and fifty nine this time I can see the brush point moving from top to bottom sometimes he says I compare my work to a very relaxed walk no hurry a slow walk from top to bottom then sideways the little finger completely tucked in the ring finger too tucked under the others the hand is a fan of folded fingers the brush tip never leaves the surface for a moment while drawing is in progress even though the figures are not joined up the movement is a cursive one whenever the arm goes to dip the brush a great sigh accompanies the face as it turns as if to avoid its own shadow or to see what's underneath it then the head's shadow shrinks and is surrounded by a halo the four lines right at the top form a little gleaming strip which seems all one colour you don't see the lines but a deposit of slightly shiny matter four million four hundred and eighty five thousand eight hundred and six with the zero six falling at the start of the line the brush is dipped elbow against side deep sigh as the hand comes back up again the wall with the recessed entrance door in the corner is largely hidden by a tall bookshelf next to which stands the glass fronted cabinet and next to that another bookshelf the same size as the first the cornice along the top of the cabinet projects above the tall rectangles of shelves on the floor in front of the furniture piles of books catalogues papers a white telephone in the first bookshelf most of the books are lying down in the other they are standing up but a record player an answering machine a radio occupy the three bottom shelves beyond the second bookshelf the wall is bare leaning against it is the *detail* in which the first million came up the hand has drawn two thirds of the line it moves forwards quickly its jerking progress punctuated by cloth rubbing four million four hundred and eighty five thousand eight hundred and fifty this time the line begins with the zero two lines higher up I was on seven hundred and fifty nine so there's been some slippage a different number of numbers per line which isn't due to my figures being bigger I must confess that when I was doing four million four hundred and eight five thousand eight hundred and thirty five I noticed I had skipped one between eight hundred and thirty two and eight hundred and thirty four so I did eight hundred and thirty two again after eight hundred and thirty five and carried on from there leaving the evidence of my mistake visible what's done is done you can't go back in time sometimes noises disturb me and draw me towards the outside I lose concentration somebody laughs in the building the space of the room suddenly slots into a larger space and its well-lit air is suspended inside a darker air when silence returns the suspension feeling wavers then the room becomes the whole of space once again I go over to sit between the corner of the second bookshelf and the million *detail* the light on the canvas seems brighter the body is different because the face is shifted to the right and the wrist and hand now seen from below form a strange curve which puts them out of alignment the way the hand bends backwards as if about to tip over gives a feeling of mutilation I can see the fingertips touching the canvas the brush between thumb and forefinger its tip dancing then jumping the line seems less cursive even though the tip does not leave the surface Opalka bends down dips the brush the hand holding the pot seems to have lost its little finger and thumb the chin drops against the chest for a few seconds then raises itself following the gaze and the right hand as they rise the face is concentrated on the gaze intent on the work zone the new line begins with an eight a five another eight a nine and a seven the hand seems to be both stuck to the canvas and struggling to escape from it on the fireplace wall another *detail* hangs opposite the million one on the floor a small television what do I see a man standing in front of a canvas a spotlamp throws a glaring light on his skull the top of which is pink amid the shining white hair the great canvas stands before him like a cinema screen the body and the screen are linked by the arm which is their common organ between the fireplace and the window wall there is a large rectangular form on the floor which might be a bed base or a low rigid sofa it is covered in bubble plastic it's the stock of prepared canvasses carefully stacked flat one on top of the other four million four hundred and eighty five thousand nine hundred and forty five I am about to start the eighth line the hand quivers engaged in a process of fertilisation while the dipping is going on I can see the tiny notch made by the current line that he says is where it's bleeding from when the hand returns to continue the line it hides the notch and the line emerges from it so is it the hand that's bleeding Opalka goes over to the fireplace cleans his brush dries it on a cloth returns to the picture goes back to work when he dips the brush his body relaxes sigh leg bent shudder of back the motion of the brush tip is highly rhythmical it joins together curves slanting horizontal and vertical lines in swift twisting movements that combine contradictory directions each number necessarily contains the same figures but the eye sees only the twisting movements like a minuscule dance linking repeated gestures together without showing any sign of the repetition are you aware of each figure as you draw it or just the number as a whole it's an unconscious process he says like writing when you write a word you don't think about the spelling you only think about the sentence and what it means the left leg is slightly bent the right very straight four million four hundred and eighty five thousand nine hundred and ninety one this time the line ends on a whole number he immediately launches himself over to the left and starts the next one it would be more appropriate he says for me to say all the numbers out loud but I only do it for part of the *detail* just to get myself used to speaking them for the time when I'll be working entirely in white suddenly the brush turns round in the hand and the tip of the handle starts scratching the canvas there's a bit of dirt stuck on here he says perhaps an insect or a lump of paint that wasn't properly ground the brush goes back to its normal position the line carries on how I ask myself how is the difference between life and work nullified here I'm seeing movements and positions are they the means of transforming everyday reality into work it is as if the body were diffusing into the canvas is not the immobility the near immobility of the body at work in order to avoid its creating its own time incompatible with the irreversible time which it experiences on the canvas here we are at four million four hundred and eighty five thousand sorry four hundred and eighty six thousand and thirty nine I've pushed the last four figures i.e. six zero and thirty nine onto the next line Opalka turns his back on the canvas and walks towards the middle of the room there's one last point he says to mention something that runs right through the implementation of my programme which is the satisfaction felt by the creator who gradually gets nearer to the completion of his undertaking and to the anxiety about his own end which will be materialised in a last unfinished *detail* that *detail* will for the first time give a finite meaning to the non finished because that ultimate meaning was anticipated from the moment I put the first number onto the canvas no other artist has ever thought of using the interruption of his work by death as something creative he goes over to the fireplace busies himself with bottle glass and pot I've added two drops of water he says because the paint was getting too thick he stirs his new mixture and resumes the confrontation with the canvas a third *detail* is propped against the window wall at the head of the stack of prepared canvasses it is to the left of the window to the right between window and door stands a drop leaf writing desk with drawers and hanging above it but nearer the door is a *travel card* in front of the desk a wooden chair what I'm doing he says is not visual poetry it's writing I'm not elevating the visual aspect the important thing for me is that the thing should function on a logical level I no longer have to ask myself how to make it the thing is made and that's it just as life makes itself I say writing because apart from the communication of a message writing is also a process which functions solely in terms of truth writing breathes out the next step in its own becoming and this breathing is the immediate proof of the process logic means that I know what I have to do but writing allows me to do it in movement but I say doesn't everyday life tend to intrude into the movement no he says lived time and clock time are not the same in here counted time doesn't exist it's out there in the world outside at that moment we only realise it is half past three because Marie-Madeleine has just stuck her head round the door to remind us that it is long past lunch time

1 May 1990/2

click click as the brush stirs the paint in the pot Opalka examines the surface I need to do a bit more retouching on my repairs he prods along the edge leans with his nose towards the canvas when you get to complete white will it be the same white he turns round yes the same while I'm still on gray the tendency is for each new background to be lighter if the weather is damp the canvas seems darker because it takes longer to dry I always prepare several at once so as to be able to correct for that effect which is why I sometimes find myself having to use one intended to come third as the first in a sequence because it is darker as a result of circumstances I said the whites would be the same yes but in the early stages you'll probably see a fairly subtle trace of one white on another which will doubtless disappear in any case I say there'll be a mark where paint has been added yes but it will only be visible with great effort or through a magnifying glass in the beginning for my preparations I had thought that all I needed to do was to keep little jars of the base paint and number them so that retouching would always be possible that's quite wrong in practice I always have to remix it for the black reduces down in the white I said one percent extra white for each new canvas now I say approximately one percent for it's impossible to be accurate I can't claim that after a hundred canvasses I'll have arrived at white on white the boundary could never be that precise a lifetime is not measured with that degree of precision either if I get to white on white i.e. to canvasses which though painted will appear blank I'll carry on working our sense of duration as life goes on means that we can carry on living at the age of ninety or a hundred we tell ourselves we can still hang on until every second I think to myself is the extreme second and its extremity is intertwined with the movements of the brush creating not its own particular duration but duration in general you have to let yourself be absorbed into the line of numbers if you are to be carried along by it and its duration made from the continual metamorphosis of the end uttered by each number which at the same time calls for the birth of the next the first million *detail* I say gives more the impression of a progression a surface yes it's not all swamped in the kind of fog that's developing now it's more plastic I say more written yes he says but the fact that the writing is more visible makes it less like a piece of writing the visible aspect dominates the journey towards the light entails the disappearance of what used to be seen as the image's perfection faced with a white piece of paper any artist might wonder can I improve on that but is doing nothing the answer no certainly not I spoke of mental white spiritual white there's no short cut to achieving that because such white is neither a blank canvas nor a monochrome one rather it's a ghost yes the ghost of the total journey which has led up to that point such a degree of patience is necessary it's indispensable he goes back to the picture examines the minor repairs to the surface high up the current line has remained open every number I think to myself is the result of all those that have gone before it just as each moment of our lives is carried along by all the others that constitute its past but no moment ever repeats an earlier one though it may be similar Opalka advances while stirring his mixture what I'm making he says is the most adequate image of life I don't think I'm crazy while my work may seem cold it is actually very moving because of that adequation to life very moving for me but I think it's the most moving thing that has ever been done there's something about it that is incredibly moving something stronger than my life it's a strength that you build up and dynamise with all your other strengths it mounts up towards an explosion will I be able to hang on and resist the pressure the things I did before can also be found in De Kooning or Soulages they contain at most a few seconds a few moments of emotion at a single sitting whereas here in the *detail* accumulation becomes the sole driving force of a whole life and it's nothing like an adventure with colour or a chapter among others the thing advances still coherent advances for the full length of a sentence without full stops or commas and which expands expands into incomparable emotion obviously I didn't invent the figures I invented what to do with them a whole universe if I think about white on white or numerical situations like seven sevens I get carried away with emotion I know that eight eights is beyond the scope of a human life however long seven sevens isn't a boundary that I have set for myself it's a symbol of my awareness of a limit seven sevens fills me with such emotion that I could drop dead on the spot it represents a situation where old age and the length of time taken to get there will make the emotion of it physically and mentally unbearable and dangerous Opalka returns to the picture leans forwards straightens again comes back over to me talking about this emotional factor I've realised something else if I do get to white on white it will happen around the turn of the millennium I didn't plan it that way from the start it's pure chance and when I say chance I have in mind that my rational method leads to certain effects which are not so obviously rational there are signs between the inside and the outside little signs which don't make me give up on rationality but force me to say that the rational and materialism are not all there is I have not given up on reason and materialism but I don't stubbornly stick to any dogmatic and therefore outdated position he has returned to the picture in the course of the last few words the hand that was stirring is now high up amid his life line it brushes the surface in gentle dabs I'm too much of a sceptic he murmurs to be just a pessimist the hand runs along suddenly enveloping itself in complete silence four million four hundred and eighty six thousand one hundred and eighty nine I'm putting the hundred and eighty nine at the beginning of the line renewed silence the hand within it when I am on my own he says and can't share my thoughts the emotion is stronger we don't like loneliness but to be really at home you need to be alone that doesn't mean I want you to go you know the hand continues writing transporting on the spot no gesturing a minimum just a face to face encounter and body flows out onto the canvas the brush tip rehashes each figure but with such assurance that each drawn detail seems immediately haloed in light no need he says to leave gaps since each number starts with two fours the body is at a slight slant deep sigh the shoulders the line of the shoulders forms a little ramp upon which the head swivels the working hand is its magnetic north four million four hundred and eighty six thousand two hundred and forty one to start with here on the left I can't see the work just a back and whatever sticks out beyond it click click sigh the hand has dipped the line accepts its additional material what is an illusion I wonder it's anything done completely without scepticism the hand seems to be drawing a little spiral on the spot the white stripe made by the lines already finished is a living surface compared to the rest of the canvas it gleams unevenly in the light as soon as I stare at it whereas at first sight it seemed uniform if I stand about a metre away I see measured writing advancing slowly calmly regularly each figure emerging from a loose movement which traces its outline with anatomical care yes which gives it an anatomy rather than analysing it the hand doesn't make gestures it overflows with them they flood forth secreting those little figures from a metre away the white stripe is populated with gray and white segments that fill it with infinite nuances but without generating arrays interlocking patterns waves such as I see if I turn my head to look at the surface of the Million *detail* so called because it contains the moment when the first million was reached the relationship of the numbers to the whole is changing all the time in this Million as if relations of proximity and distance were constantly being permuted I move over to examine the *detail* near the window which is the latest to be painted and which contains the number four million four hundred and forty four thousand four hundred and forty four from close up its surface seems to be composed of interlocking trapeziums from further away and only after looking hard because at first it seems just a blur I notice a resemblance to the Million but a discreet internal one which leaves the eye restlessly seeking a stable point of view on this world where there are no fixed shapes and everything constantly slides together despite the fact that it is made up of lines one above the other four million four hundred and eighty six thousand four hundred and thirty eight I've put the eight at this end i.e. the beginning only here the lines seem to have fused with the surface I count them one by one and not without difficulty because they become mixed up at the end the total is five hundred and thirteen I've never done that Opalka says while watching me count but it's not for me to do it to start with I didn't intend to write or say anything about my work however I had to intervene because it was generating too many misunderstandings fortunately I'm free of the trap of novelty all I need to do is work in the same way just as the body knows it wants to go on living the telephone rings Opalka picks up the receiver and answers he talks about preparations for the Mont-de-Marsan exhibition I hear what he says while being determined not to listen and go over to the Million to count the lines this time they are clearer more distinctly placed one below the other the total is four hundred and thirty two the difference between this and the other one is considerable eighty one lines maybe I've miscounted by a hundred Opalka is saying how tired his legs are as he has only started painting again today after a long break for his trip to Germany and preparing for the exhibition and yet he says what a pleasure it is to be doing what I am doing my doubts force me to go and count the lines on the third *detail* the one opposite the Million which was painted just before the seven fours there is the same blurring effect five hundred and seven lines which seems to confirm the seven fours total even when the lines are clearly delineated as in the Million picture the effect is not linear because what you see are interlocking blocks eddies and swirls when no linearity is detectable as in the two latest *details* the visual effect is that of a surface the comparison between the numbers of lines leads Opalka to remark in the Million the frequency of ones might have led me to make the lines wider I try to keep it the same all the time which isn't strictly the case but it is relatively I work with the general idea that my lines are five millimetres wide if I only do four it leads to a huge difference the glasses are perhaps the problem because they make things seem bigger in any case I say you aren't cheating by cutting down the quantity of numbers as you progress quite the opposite and already I am working out the number of numbers in the Million it begins with nine hundred and ninety three thousand nine hundred and sixty and ends with one million eleven thousand eight hundred and seventy five which comes out at seventeen thousand nine hundred and fifteen numbers the last completed *detail* but one starts with four million four hundred and fifteen thousand six hundred and fifty nine and ends on four million four hundred and thirty nine thousand eight hundred and fifteen which gives twenty four thousand one hundred and fifty six numbers as for the seven fours it begins with four million four hundred and thirty nine thousand eight hundred and sixteen and ends with four million four hundred and sixty five thousand and fifty four making twenty six thousand eight hundred and thirty eight numbers i.e. six to seven thousand more in the most recent *details* this number count is obviously just a way of knocking on the door of the painter's work in the knowledge that there is no way of opening it other than the work itself with no illusions here for once writing has come to the surface and in so doing has spread time out through space and blurred the old dimensions by sending abroad the quiver of a generalised presence that changes the quality of the world

2 May 1990

the *detail* there in the light the white band is a substance whose surface is full of irregularities you can make out not figures but nodules I'm up to four million four hundred and eighty six thousand four hundred and eighty seven I'm leaving the two fours over on the right and starting again with the rest it's no accident that I fill up right to the edge without leaving the slightest empty space if I had been stupid enough to leave a margin I would have been producing an aesthetic object contemporary art always has an element of showmanship things I find rather fake it's a kind of pollution we have crap foisted upon us and we glory in it Opalka moves away from his picture as he speaks he has brush and pot in hand he comes a few steps forwards he criticises Kieffer for bluffing with his very large pictures if you scream into a powerful PA you can shout everyone else down he returns abruptly to his picture the hair glints in the light the brush is working away just below the ear and rules a line through the row of little hillocks on the hand the right shoulder comes forward and hides the work only the back remains a sort of airy silence a creak the left shoulder shudders clearing of throat in the gray shadow cast on the left side of the canvas a cartouche of light ringed with black appears it's a reflection from one lens of his glasses the working hand reappears above the right shoulder the tip of the brush handle describes a tiny circle next to the shirt collar the right elbow moves against the side deep sigh I listen out for the sound of the wrist rubbing on the canvas and as I can't hear it I suddenly feel certain that this work secretes silence the hand hides behind the head my gaze runs up against the skull a wrinkle starts at the top of the left shoulder and runs under the right armpit standing out in relief the right hand emerges slowly below the ear moves forwards a little revealing the brush handle which twitches the right arms drops the shoulder and neck draw back defining on the canvas a curved space in the hollow of which appears the small damp shine of the line Opalka walks over to the fireplace pours a little paint into his pot stirs it click click then straight back to work the right hand above the right shoulder higher this time complete independent and pulling along in its direction the head which points in line with its slow progress a weird organ armed with a little lance but what a lot of lines all of a sudden the collar the wrinkle the handle the belt the left sleeve the jeans pockets what a lot of lines which combine to compose the space with the upper horizontal of the picture and its two verticals a body made of surfaces and contours so we're up to four million four hundred and eighty six thousand five hundred and eighty five and I've only got the eighty five on the left Opalka turns round on the subject of the lines I wanted to tell you that I started by leaving more space between the numbers horizontally and vertically then I realised that there was no point because the last figure changes all the time and you immediately pick up the start of the next number the first and last figures create a gap in this work you get your method from experience and habit without even thinking about it from the very first *detail* I tended not to leave gaps that's why the whole thing is like a single sentence without commas or full stops it's a unit with no gaps which produces a single meaning between the number I am writing and the very first there is a constant relationship just as there is a constant relationship between the present and the beginning of our lives we are continually separating from ourselves and reuniting with ourselves there is perpetual change and an unbroken relationship with our birth and even with conception in our mother's womb we never escape from that relationship just as my work never escapes from its movement it's an image of life what is time it's movement and life movement again people often say to me it can't be too tiring doing what you do of course it is but it also gives me a strength that carries me along long marches exhaust you but they also buoy you up our past carries us along in the same way but our memory forgets it whereas in my work there is no forgetting there is just the manifestation of a single movement which forgets nothing Opalka has abruptly gone back to facing the picture motionless and brightly lit he has never emerged from his silence and the light he is back in his own world and I see his solitude inside and out solitude in the light a fundamental isolation something impersonal living within the self the opposite of a dark fate an illuminated fate which does not drive you deeper into yourself but puts you outside in the clear light the brush is above the shoulder spinning off its movement which the hand cocoons advancing inexorably the telephone rings hello yes I'm working I take advantage of the chance to take a closer look at the quarry face the open vein line twenty one so little space between the numbers a breath of air in everything I do he says on the telephone there's no danger of repetition I'm always doing the same thing but it's always different the twenty one lines are made up of strips of matter you'll have noticed he says after putting the phone down that I've stopped at twenty three interruptions and mistakes they all make you think he falls silent or rather into silence once more the stone walls the carpet the overall harmony are the substance of this silence sigh the right leg flexes straightens the brush handle sticks out from the collar have you worked out what makes the little noise Opalka turns round it's this rubbing he points to his wrist in the film they dubbed it as the noise of the brush which is absurd precisely I say this morning I noticed that it makes no noise at all he goes back to work I listen and watch the hand nibbling away at space a noise of rumpled cloth the handle follows the ridge of the shoulder and the shoulder moves along behind it the strip already painted would look like a surface if the rest of the picture did not underline its narrowness from a distance the whole strip looks the same shade of white from close up there are greys and paler patches so we're on four million four hundred and eighty six thousand six hundred and sixty nine the last five figures starting the new line I am tempted to count how often whole or split numbers fall at the end of lines nothing is insignificant in a *detail* because every indication leads back to the origin even at the risk of losing itself there the moment when the visible is engulfed by the invisible is also a representation of the invisible Opalka goes over to the fireplace pours some paint into the pot stirs the mixture the last twenty five lines of the Million contain eleven splits but there seem to be more whole numbers near the bottom in the middle I find fourteen in twenty seven lines which is practically the same the hand is once again above the shoulder there is a hole between thumb and forefinger the head rotates in the middle of a sigh the phone rings hello silence hangs up would you believe it some crap sales pitch already back at work the reflector hides head and shoulders sigh click click corner of forehead and glasses no socks this morning when the hand is working the right heel is out of its clog there we are four million four hundred and eighty six thousand seven hundred and twenty but I'll leave the forty four over there and start here with the eighty six thousand seven hundred and twenty of the first twelve lines of the *detail* eight begin with a four it is very hard to concentrate on the beginning of a line and isolate it it blurs into those around it and the blurring spreads it out into a flat surface a space there we are four million four hundred and eighty six thousand seven hundred and seventy one and again I've got two fours over on the right that's the third time I'm having a lot of trouble I say seeing the beginnings of lines it's easier he says doing what I do than decoding the relations you know what they are but you can't see them because you're swimming in the middle of them upon which he is already back at work with no transition and this gives an impression of absolute continuity which I note with the same astonishment for the twentieth time this morning outside it's a fine day green leaves and blue sky I turn my back on them to look at Opalka whose back is turned to me what is the Other in relation to this imperturbable image of life constructing itself line by line an awareness of uselessness destroys any illusion the hand is resting on the canvas the index and middle fingers are scarcely moving they conceal the bristles of the brush this time the line ends on a completed four million four hundred and eighty six thousand eight hundred and twenty three Opalka immediately moves left eye nose mouth ear in profile details which once noted lead the eye upwards chin curls above and below the ear arm elbow wrist hand handle little rubbing sound sigh hand drawn back rubbing sound moves forwards the pot rotates in the left hand while the right dives in for a dip head first pulls out again sigh breathing which rubs the air as the hand does the canvas as if some cloth in space some thickening of the invisible medium what rigidity suddenly in the vigilant profile in its tension a sigh undercuts it and it collapses only to return as soon as the hand touches starts nibbling advancing leaving behind its damp trail the fine tip of bristle turns twirls twirls so finely that right and left top and bottom are threaded together by the line twists and turns and zigzags generate breadth and height linearity explodes spreads out into a surface the shadow of the forearm with its rolled up shirt cuff makes a black phallus from which springs the shadow hand advancing in tandem with the hand of flesh above it the virtual body accompanies the real one nothing is separate any longer here experience reigns it has eliminated representation the witness tries doggedly to follow the movements to see what it is that they are infusing into the numbers the arm moves the elbow turns the gaze leaves them to go and rub up against the surface of the Million where it touches infinity in the profusion of possible vectors here another whole number four million four hundred and eighty six thousand eight hundred and seventy two but already life is continuing on the other side neutralising the extremity at the moment when it comes up against it for the thing it infuses is continuity what is this way of advancing whose penetration leaves behind it not only that which it penetrates but also the moment of penetration itself to produce continuity there is nothing in front of us nothing but the infinite carried along at each moment by the finite constantly shifting constantly generating a non-finitude which is the opening of the finite onto infinity and what then is the end towards which leads the never finished finitude of the hand adding one figure to another finishing a number and passing on immediately to the non-finitude of the next what is the extremity perpetually there but pushed back millimetre by millimetre the bristle tip works revolves unspins the end from the end returns to dip itself in matter and resumes the continuity inexhaustible and yet without illusion because every end contains within its here and now the elsewhere of before and the elsewhere of afterwards the neck tilted back a little the hand once again close to the edge the elbow animated twitching gently so four hundred and forty eight to the right and six thousand nine hundred and twenty on the left head thrust forwards eye opened wide in the profile hand raised hand working as if its were the only permanence a grimace on the face or perhaps wrinkles exaggerated by the light tension in the neck below the angle of the chin the foot comes up the cheek scratches itself on the brush handle all these bottles annoy you he says turning round and his gaze scrutinises me before returning to the picture and that moment is drowned in silence the hand floats high up in front of the profile in front of the light do you I ask do you always wait for the end of a number before you dip the brush oh yes he says always always except when there's an interruption the phone ringing for instance this time he hasn't turned round the hand has stayed at its place of work has it made progress it's moving along now with its little swaying mast now I put four four eight and six on the right and start again with nine hundred and sixty eight the hand leans on the first knuckles of thumb and forefinger and presses with the middle finger against the fleshy bulge it's a crouching animal which from time to time does a little leap to the right the hand has two parts one which moves all the time twitching and nibbling the other fat and fleshy which occasionally makes a minute jump here I've made a mistake can you believe it I was on eighty nine and instead of doing ninety I put seventy the visual movement of the nine created a reaction towards the seven I'll transfer over here four million four hundred and eighty six thousand nine hundred and eighty nine and repeat the numbers from four million four hundred and eighty six thousand nine hundred and seventy to nine hundred and eighty four but why stop I say at nine hundred and eighty four since you were on nine hundred and eighty nine because it was when I was on eighty four that I noticed the relationship with the previous line was wrong the difference had gone up to fourteen which is impossible so I looked for the cause and discovered the mistake in life when you find you've got it wrong you can't go back because time is irreversible but mistakes teach us things yes they teach us a lesson there he says leaning towards the surface there is a sort of confession in the moral sense when I've got to white on white I won't be able to express that visually any longer he has turned to face me while talking about white and then gone back to work and silence surrounds him he leans his head onto the right shoulder then jerks it over to the left prolonged rubbing noise which fills the ear with the presence of cloth confession I said silence the voice hesitates confession not in the religious sense but in the Jean-Jacques Rousseau sense because there's an element of the diary in my story the hand continues it's a hand that writes the whole time a hand that works like breathing like the heart beating the gaps between numbers form slanting lines never vertical ones these slanting lines bend in the Million picture to produce strange effects of height and depth which are absent from the seven fours and the previous picture in which I can see only surface and fog do you have a rule for when you stop intentionally not at all I just make sure I've finished the last number do you have a rule for the amount of paint that can be left on the brush no no rule the body's shadow breathes on the surface ah well this time I'm calling it a day on four million four hundred and eighty seven thousand and ninety three

24 February 1996

it's the *detail* containing the number with seven fours in says Opalka gesturing over to the right towards the far end of the room the gaze searches for signs a certain configuration the current *detail* is in the centre on the easel watched over by two microphones one to the right the other to the left slender animals rearing up the same reflectasol on its stand still towers over the tape recorder it breaks up the view partially concealing the current *detail* very monumental yes a massive monument gleaming in the light almost white in the part already painted the white is alive vibrant making the section still blank seem almost gray Opalka stands in front of it long dark gray woollen jacket to the observer sitting on the floor and looking up the line in progress is on a level with his neck five million ninety one thousand seven hundred and thirty seven upper body in partial profile right shoulder towards the picture working hand and arm invisible for the moment left arm bent holding the glass with paint in slight shift backwards both elbows move white collar beneath white hair sigh bright light on the canvas the reflectasol cuts off the top of the skull and stands out whiter against the white surface cough there's a bouquet lying in the hearth seven pink and white tulips the working hand and arm are still concealed by the shoulder the hand must be working at face height shift to the left start of a new line the hand is on top of the shoulder it is nothing but a fist a triangle of a fist moving very slowly in a rotating motion the fist vanishes brush knocking against glass the whole torso shudders the fist reappears on the shoulder the tip of the elbow moves against the body it won't be long before you start feeling chilly even though the temperature's all right Opalka turns walks towards the corner of the bookshelves announces nineteen comes back over to the canvas three fingers clenched around the brush the working hand hides its thumb arching its back like a little naked animal ruminating or nibbling deep sigh slight creaking from parquet or clogs the hand runs behind the woollen collar the bouquet casts a shadow of just three flowers on the fireback the bench is still there behind it leaning against the wall a voluminous stack of blank canvasses at the window end of the bench in the corner three finished *details* wrapped in glassine paper and five million ninety one thousand eight hundred and twenty four do you paint the numbers or write them I paint them because I'm a painter but the ambiguity about writing is always there what I do could have been done as a book if I were a writer I would have stuck to *travel cards* but since I'm a painter and I wanted to remain one I paint I once said about the sequence of numbers that I was painting my existence now I also say that what I paint is painting itself which I agree is a rather shorthand account of my enterprise but what's your point of view on the painting writing ambiguity I didn't want to limit myself to painting and just do art for art's sake I didn't feel that painting was enough perhaps because I took my role in society too seriously what do you do once you've acquired the basics of the business I picked them up between forty-nine and fifty-six precisely the years of Stalinism then came the thaw and the uprisings when I left school I knew I was hooked on being a painter even if I could have chosen something else hooked by the universe of painting which had become my reason for living in the Stalinist times painters were regarded as engineers of the human soul which was confirmation of the artist's social role after fifty-six we had a degree of freedom again in the visual arts at least but there was no market we were able to exhibit in a few galleries specialising in abstract art which was almost official art in Poland then came happenings conceptual art no problems even some positive reviews in the press the Sixties gave me complete freedom precisely because there was no market over there here where the free market makes anything possible there is definitely less real freedom there I was free to ask myself the question what shall I do in a society that expects nothing of me I could have earned my living drafting posters but I wanted to remain a painter and act like a painter that forced me to think hard about painting and what I was expecting of myself you need to be aware that life is of little importance but that little must prove the quality of uselessness communist society produced in order to produce nothing produced non-existent rabbits as Ehrenburg used to say the cult of production and proving yourself through work were part of the absurdity of that society of course among the artists there were a few greasy individuals who sucked up to the Party but after fifty-six that was no longer compulsory in capitalist countries you don't see what you should be seeing because everything is distorted by consumption in a socialist society TV was much more interesting because of the plays and films here an artist has no time to take his time time to do nothing walking has become my profession numbers are the steps in my walk which has been going on since nineteen sixty-five walking leaves you time to meet up with your own thought not like those artist joggers who are always running after the market and the latest trend an artist in countries like France or America could never manage my kind of thinking well there are a few examples On Kawara Hanne Darboven are also thinking artists but they each have a sort of obsession Kawara's is with the calendar Darboven has a big thing about archives what interests me is real time its movement its dynamics and its duration whether it's the twenty fourth or twenty fifth makes no difference the date matters for going to collect you from the station but not for the emotion of being Darboven and Kawara operate in an arbitrary way on a specific moment in time whereas for me the canvas is a universe a presence a being manifesting its existence an egotistical insanity with a universal relevance I'm bearing witness not just to my life but to life in general in my canvas you can see a presence an emotion I don't narrate short-lived current events I am painting a single body I'm painting the big bang if Kawara wants to have a press pack on his date painting that's up to him I have nothing in common with that arbitrary sticking of a pin into the calendar what interests me is the flow of time and my defiance of it in the context of death as a celebration of life I wanted first and foremost to be and remain a painter I wanted to save painting because it's one of the all time greatest qualities invented by man I took the idea of saving painting literally and tried to prove that with a stretcher and some canvas you could still do something worth doing I resolved to stick within the image of a painter standing before his canvas and painting the essence of painting which is contained within that synthesis and I refused to go outside that space in order to prove that within its limits you could create a dynamic that had little to do with painting from the past each of my *details* is part of *a whole* the first sign marks the start of the genetic development of a body which is perpetually being finished the fact that there is already enough being to finish with gives me an opening a freedom when I enter my studio I enter a state where a being is finishing and dying and I am gripped by an emotion which is an exaltation of life rather than of death life may be of little consequence but awareness of that little makes it glorious the finite defined by the non finite that notion and therefore that emotion have never before been painted I have given painting the ability to go beyond a skull or a portrait I don't paint my own face but rather the emotion of being and I've given painting a dimension which is new compared to everything that used to constitute novelty in painting the Marxist theorists were right to say that it's the idea that must seek a form that's a fortunate thing for painting nobody can paint figures after me it looks as if I'm closing things off but the reverse is true it's an invitation not to continue my work by imitation but to see it differently not in haste jogging past you need to stop and stake your life it's life and life alone that has value and not some imitation of youth contemporary artists have put themselves in a position where all value resides in youth they are like politicians jumping up and down and even dancing on the podium because they're ashamed of their age as if only young artists were capable of being inventive and then came retirement in art there's nothing that can be done better all you can do is go deeper into things it's a well known fact that old painters paint more profoundly in the sense of their awareness of what they're doing even if their hand shakes my approach adds a different quality in Paris I met a doctor who said to me looking at your exhibition makes me wish I were older that's just an image when I think of death I think of my œuvre completed I'm not making any bets with Lucifer to stay young like Faust I'm betting with death for my œuvre a sort of checkmate with death for my œuvre this checkmate image reminds me of Duchamp who played chess as a retirement hobby my approach also checkmates Duchamp for him it's over for me it's just beginning Duchamp artistic gimmicks moustaches on the Mona Lisa a move you can understand intellectually but culturally deplorable just like burning down a church or museum he didn't do it on the canvas itself but it's the same thing a sure sign of intelligence but very irresponsible you can't go around smashing your own place up sooner or later every cultural gesture has consequences the Mona Lisa what hasn't been done to that poor picture it's been defiled in all sorts of ways you don't rape young girls you shouldn't interfere with our heritage it's the proof of our human quality we mustn't accept the past being turned into a circus caricature we need to look at it critically not invent a new barbarism we are destroying our culture for the media nothing is sacred any more the Mona Lisa isn't sacred in herself but the object is Empedocles said that from time to time a god turns up here on Earth Leonardo was one of them towering above anything that has been produced since you can't imitate quality when Leonardo drew a machine or a woman he immediately became a god he might well have been fascinated by electronics but the sheer quality of his hand makes us ask questions about all this virtuality aren't we going to lose the miracle of a creative interplay between hand and mind people have often said to me but come on Roman you could do that with a machine Fréchuret got it right when he wrote in his book "Machines à peindre" ("Painting Machines") that I was the only one of those contemporary artists who might be compared to a painting machine who was actually not one but in fact the perfect counter-example to it people allow themselves to be misled by their first contact how can a work provide art with a new *raison d'être* while still taking its place in art history it all depends on how I project myself beyond my œuvre in time can a work like mine and its approach its pictorial sacrifice provide an energy with which to fight visual pollution can it help to save art through its emotion alone I think that no other work of art has ever given off so much emotion as mine does I am not playing a role I am I glorify my existence my presence in this universe egotistical folly perhaps but to create an image of each one of us I paint painting how could you give an extra dimension to painting to me a bit of graffiti on a canvas is an anecdote no more than an illustration we need to rethink the imagination the way we imagine the imagination has generally become stunted bourgeois I think of the imagination on a quite different scale a cosmic scale you're wearing me out trying to keep up with what you're saying I'll get back to my painting off he goes the hand on top of the shoulder the back very straight in the light but almost immediately about turn oh before I forget I imagined the number one could set everything going like a big bang I imagined one as being like Malevich's black square black on black and from there I imagined that Malevich checkmated himself he'd touched on a symbolic dimension of such power when he painted his square that he couldn't eat or drink for a week which means he didn't know what to do next me when I painted my one it was an opening it gave painting an opportunity to revitalise itself from nineteen sixty-five onwards I defined something which perpetually revitalises itself developing and getting more profound all the time the imaginary dimension is constantly revitalised due to my use of death as a tool in the creation of the work I love life as much as anyone women good food but I want to know who is sitting down at table and with what kind of imagination we all know there's lots wrong with the world and it's getting worse I've never been tempted to play the clown he agitates his brush stirring the white paint returns to the picture the hand appears on top of the shoulder the brush sticking out of it and moving like a little pendulum after you'd painted one did you stop or did two follow straight away he turns quickly round haven't I told you about that already I was overcome with emotion a birth had just occurred a genesis the genesis of a life my own and now I knew that it had the ability to go further than painting had ever gone before neither abstract nor figurative an embodiment even before I had painted the sign one I was in a state of exaltation about the birth I am a painter of the body embodiment is what makes an object develop with increasing power I was aware that the progression of numbers would give that power I know that by using numbers rather than lines or colours I'm painting an image of painting itself why numbers and not dots as in the *Chronomes* because the amount of dots will always be arbitrary you have to understand the imaginative state of an artist trying to paint infinity once you look at it in terms of the projection in time of a work you can appreciate the reason for my choice and understand the nerve it takes to say I paint painting if I say it over dinner people won't understand that I'm justified in saying it or why it is that I paint my own existence I paint painting I've got good historical reasons for saying that it's life speaking about my emotion and as far as my approach is concerned there's also the question of expiation expiation of the magnificent folly of contemporary art realising that you can't tamper with values lightly they wanted to burn down the Louvre that was Le Corbusier I think but what impoverishment a world full of nothing but machines for living he didn't want to do it literally but saying it is already doing it a brutal murder to think that it has no effect because it's fictitious is utterly irresponsible you need to keep a hold on responsibility everything has its importance even if it's only minimal or else nothing does when I think back to the *Chronomes* the problem was always when on earth to stop a dot more a dot less how to decide the time that fascinates me is not calendar time or clock time but the time of emotion the instant as Kierkegaard called it the emotion of painting something that has a duration of its own except that you can always go back to a drawing or a picture I stopped doing that sort of painting in sixty-three I didn't want to get into monochrome trouble I realised that the human mind is incapable of painting chaos it immediately starts to build an organisation in what I had been doing up to then there were the beginnings of a relationship but no time arrow no logical reason so when is a canvas finished I wanted to liberate myself from arbitrariness we are caught in our destiny between an arbitrary origin and an arbitrary end but between the two there is something tightly defined without much room for choice people might sometimes think my work is a form of slavery yes maybe if we are slaves to our own lives how can we give our lives a dimension that limits their arbitrariness to an anecdote that's what I've succeeded in doing with the sequence of numbers a finite diagonal from the first number to the last something finished within the domain of the non finite when I come in here and carry on painting I am back on my walk I don't have to think about improving I think life Cézanne another picture another mountain it's not thinking about painting it's the emotion of painting Morandi painted the pictorial sensibility I'm full of admiration but as soon as you see several of them together you see a number of little gems but not the emotion of a single whole the problem of painting one picture then another was what I found difficult I wanted to paint a work in which each canvas carried the whole thing along and dynamised it the mark I make with my sequence of numbers is a positive one I want something that gives presence my canvas even when it has become white white with a well-deserved whiteness a mental white will have little in common with monochromes as we know them today it won't be just one more monochrome incidentally the monochrome is one of the most extraordinary inventions of the twentieth century I'm thinking of course of Yves Klein but also Rodchenko the pioneer and here again how can I make my ghost into the bearer of the whole I'm thinking of Van Gogh his portrait with severed ear we know exactly what he did before and after it's in the imaginary space generated by the image if you come across one of my *details* it evokes one idea and one only the presence of a stretch of time its painted presence what I paint is my consciousness you have to paint not what you are seeing when you look but what you are thinking and why do it at all that's the essential question why do it when we're weighed down by guilt that art has become a commodity he stirs his white walks over to the picture already working himself into the painting posture his body already absorbed in a continuity its duration without gaps except for the diversions the anecdotes we fit in which are not real moments but merely asides the hand stands out clearly now its clenched index and middle fingers almost hiding the thumb head held straight but tilted slightly backwards with its crown of white hair an equivalence between head and hand maybe due to their common skin colour the movement nibbles away at its allotted task clings to the edge then transports itself across to the other side and submerges itself again in its duration now the reflectasol hides the head and the upper part of the hand the cable hangs down from the camera several coughs which reverberate in the silence and make you more aware of it the room is white full of white air which mists over where it touches the bookshelves and the glass cabinet lined up against the wall where the door is there must be one more set of shelves than before the number of documents and catalogues stacked up has increased the hand appears round the fringe of the reflectasol Opalka walks towards the fireplace sound of footsteps returns stands back brush in hand bristles touching a tissue then brush in paint glass sound of pouring water and breathing head down turns back to face the picture the hand opens up then clenches again the brush tip appears for a few seconds the fingertips quiver gently the elbow moves and now the shoulder but this movement collapses in on itself and dies the hand is duplicated by a thin shadow return to the fireplace whose narrow ledge acts as a store water pouring I have the most minimal palette there is my whole approach is to work towards absolute white which doesn't mean the disappearance of everything that has been painted Leonardo called it a sfumato I'm painting the sfumato of an existence that's what I mean by saying I paint painting in his *Treatise on Painting* there's an amazing text I've photocopied it it's as if he's speaking to me here read the bit beginning "now" yes that's it now the first degree of shading is the shadow and the last the light so you must paint the darkest shadow close to its cause and make its extremity blend into light so that in other words it appears unbounded while I've been reading the current line has moved closer to the edge when the hand dips into the glass to collect paint the fingers busily stirring head aslant to look at the line consider it then straight once more as the hand carries on with its task with little bowing gestures salutations in the fingertips start of the next line brilliant white standing out against the painted part a damp and nuanced white I have to say that I have put painters back on their feet and thinking starts with verticality a painter's picture is his world and he stands vertically in front of it what you see here is an installation which includes everything necessary for carrying out a programme the most appropriate and pictorial means which function in relation to the history of painting let's suppose the spirits of different painters could communicate across the ages and they talked to each other in images as they looked at what they had each done if I were to meet Leonardo or Rembrandt or the other painters I admire and we sat down together at table they could all say to me I understand what you are doing all it would take is for each of them to have followed the development of painting it's quite logical Leonardo was proud of his little vine but on another level he was in touch with universal matters he writes to a prince I can make war machines and also paint and what do you do I'm a painter what type of painting neither figurative nor abstract so what kind is it then I see in the eyes of the person I'm talking to that he thinks I'm mad the biggest problem isn't taxi drivers or people sitting next to you in the plane it's the pretentious know-alls who think they understand why do it I regard painting as having the same reason for existing as existence itself life isn't much but it's all there is and it's no accident when I say I'm painting my life my emotion at existing he stirs violently walks towards the picture suddenly complete calm descends and spreads across the whole world the cable release dangles in front of the crease of the elbow three fingers folded under the brush handle like the pointer of a sundial its shadow shifting with the different shapes of the figures its track moves very slowly from right to left in the course of its minute oscillations it's the hand's pendulum the head bows when the hand goes for more white and both come back up together a bit of shadow precedes the movement the right leg stretches making an acute angle then returns to the vertical four heavy steps towards the fireplace click click scraping noise back to the picture profile at the bottom of which the chin juts out let me refer you to the Montagne Sainte-Victoire a mountain as large as life itself it's a real feat to climb to the top you can't come down you can only stay up there this said facing the middle of the room half way from the fireplace after which back to work then about turn large or small that depends on your point of view I'm keen to talk about what I call the quality of uselessness we are swamped with utilitarian things art itself has become useful but not mine what is man's sacred value what arguments are there for saving him what artists and poets have always tried to get the world to understand is man's quality what criterion could there be for the utility of art none in the utilitarian sense there could only be one if societies understood what is at stake and then they would need to put their resources into becoming more and more humane you can say that God is dead Art is dead but if so then what can possibly rescue the ship of humanity we're in a kind of Noah's Ark amidst a flood of stupid images it's a drug more and more stupidity on a world-wide scale that can do terrible damage to the history of mankind anyone can talk but if everyone does you can't hear what anyone's saying if you want to speak you need to prove what you are saying otherwise your truth is only a pseudo-truth or anecdote if I want to save humanity it's so that there should still be reasons for existing to be proud of our verticality my practice is an invitation to meditate on that thing we call life there are too many art objects produced and above all too many ideas on art people need time to get their breath back in the old days the public were prepared for us now we are on the fringes and there's no way we can make them share our emotion a mountaineer is climbing for everyone that's something people understand the climber has determination and courage people share his emotion project themselves into it my approach has certain things in common with climbing he turns and walks over to the picture silence some birds screech the hand advances with little jerks it is just at the level of the ear in the curve of the hair white verticality now the hand is in the hollow of the chin the brush handle appears to be scratching the collar slight twist in the torso the hand disappears behind the shoulder the left hand holds the glass level with the right elbow click click cough deep breath throat cleared he takes his jacket off and throws it on the ground I'm too hot probably got a slight temperature again I'll put a little waistcoat on it's a little blue waistcoat which makes a large crease over the right shoulder the head disappears behind the reflectasol our cretinisation through images is the fault of advertising and its attempts to generate rivalry if advertising were banned that might change things a lot but as drawing crowds is the name of the game everyone flocks towards the stupid things which incidentally are beautifully presented it's a poison we've overdosed on images I've got nothing against images though it depends what sort he cleans his brush with a tissue picks up the glass from the ledge round the fireplace shoulders in profile face in profile hair brightly lit states put massive resources into the fight against drugs they ought to do the same for culture states are rich enough to choose to bring the things that matter into the public eye he turns to face the picture stands with back tensed nape of neck upright the working hand barely projects beyond the cheek you can't plead in the name of culture but you can in the name of a balanced society the face turned round for a moment but has now become invisible again gone back to its confrontation with the picture the fingers holding the brush nibble away at the space around it I remember when they made the film about me the director timed everything very precisely he said people absolutely had to realise that I was a man just like any other so I should walk around and drink coffee I protested that we had no time to waste we needed to stick to showing the glory of painting because people are tired of what's generally on offer and a guy who's odd enough to paint numbers while calling them out must be more interesting than the usual banal stuff the chin has stayed resting on the shoulder during this reminiscence now he returns to the picture the brush hand makes a ball up against the chin the handle wiggles near the right ear an idea needs to find its man the Marxists forgot about man because they blotted out death but the emotion of life has no other point of reference than death he turns round advances two steps his right arm is folded across the chest his left dangles with the hand on the end clutching the paint glass I had calculated that I would reach absolute white around the age of seventy five which is the average life expectancy in Europe but setting up exhibitions and the necessity of explaining my work mean that I've put it back to eighty imagine an old man still indulging in rock climbing human life is defined by death no other animal has that awareness my painting is thought out like something that develops it's a life discovering it's own *raison d'être* creating is what I manage to say about what I have done both in my work and in my life before I hadn't understood the I paint painting parable it took me some time telling myself that creation is what you say about what you have done in both work and life you're bringing in a third person yes that's right a third person I am confronted by the Other Lévinas's Other I'm thinking of the need to share things with others the reason Van Gogh wrote his famous letters was to share his emotion if I speak and write it's in order to share something that's linked to the whole history of art but people need someone to tell them how it works what I'm offering is an adventure which makes waves something disturbing aggressive this violence isn't directed against anyone it's just an attack on contemporary creation through the problems it raises I've given the avant-gardes a hard time for example by stressing embodiment despite my conceptual approach or being stubbornly determined to stay within painting which made people assume I was a traditionalist which isn't true because I've used traditional means to call into question both painting and the avant-garde it might sound pretentious but my ladder runs from Altamira to Opalka the scandal I'm causing is comparable to Duchamp's urinal but I am an anti-Duchamp and that's what's shaken and shocked the joggers who go for visual gimmicks can pissing be art it's bad to piss in our places of refuge my work is collective as well as individual I regard that as crucial I feed on the emotion which comes from the participation of others the climber climbs alone but he knows that other people know you work within a collective movement people can understand a discourse a logic a meaning as long as you maintain your relationship to an idea if I had changed shirts the whole time I would have produced not an image of time but a collection of shirts what I display isn't a narcissistic image but the image of a head that imagines goes deeper into things to start with I didn't take any photos each photo marks the parabola between the one before and the next you have to be able to think through the *raison d'être* and provide proof the artist's role is also to be a point of reference for a certain way of living his culture starts when he sits down to eat and continues through his visual surroundings I don't cut myself off from the world I answer the telephone I'm open to things that might disturb me I've set myself up here to avoid the obligations of city living the daily social round no problem I answer I'm no monk my approach couldn't work if I were isolated from the world normally when I shave in the morning I listen to the news what's happening in the world I have lunch at one so I can watch the news it's the only thing on television that interests me despite the distortions I want to know what everybody else is being told the information they are given how they're being manipulated the same thing again at eight p.m. then I come back up to work unless there's someone visiting it's the opposite of cutting yourself off from the world standing there in front of my canvas with the verticality of the painter I feel much better adapted to the world than I would caught up in the contemporary race it seems to me that my position is much more appropriate than all that frantic gesticulating in so-called harmony with this crazy world what I do and why I do it I wanted to make people see themselves seeing it could only be done through painting there's the idea of a thermodynamic image it all started with my awareness of the inadequacy of random chance because there's no way of finishing you need to define the end and the way to do that is by using death as the definition of the work that's the diabolical side of what I do the arrow of time goes in all directions there's a direction towards infinity which invents itself through linearity just like our lived experience our memory that's what I bring out in my installations which I arrange so as to have sound mingling with every layer of the programme I make a point of recording each transition to the next million but the fifth for instance is in the same general ambience as the rest I tried this installation experiment for the first time in São Paulo in a space of at least four hundred square metres I arranged five sound sources which created a sort of dialogue within unity a dialogue inside a monologue I organised it with complete freedom as happens in our memory this sonic dimension is like the varnish on a canvas the sound creates a unity that's what an installation is instead of going into a space with pictures in you enter a picture it's a very intimate penetration almost a rape because there's a strong bodily aspect you're entering my life you can see and feel this dimension it's obvious I had to go through a learning experience that was completed in Venice I never do the same thing twice I redynamise the same thing you don't live in order to grow old but to learn what you are able to learn different spaces have taught me many things as I have moved from exhibition to exhibition around Europe one after the other each space has forced me to be more demanding in Venice knowing that a lot was expected of me I worked for a whole month to create the finest space of my life I hope that one day I'll have the opportunity to create a space that will last for ever thanks to these installations I have discovered that a space is a creation certain principles have to be respected and each time you need to find the appropriate solution for the place I wanted it to be self-evident that it could only be like that and no other way doing an installation is a kind of feast day within my project curators have to give me spaces instead of just hanging my pictures any old way in Munich Helmut Friedel created a disaster with three of my canvasses you can't hang my *details* like ordinary pictures you need to etablish a meaning between *details* photos and sound because space is a creation you can give me the most awful space and I'll transform it one evening I was having dinner with one of my oldest friends a man of complete integrity and a real art enthusiast I'm talking about that extraordinary chap Alain Julien Laferrière who was kind enough to invite Christian Schlatter and me to do the first in his series of Grand Lectures in Tours he said to me Roman there must be something wrong with you you want to take care of everything yourself you don't leave anything up to the curators he was going to give a talk and he'd prepared a sort of picture rail and was intending to hang a *detail* on it that's no good I said you can't do that and in fifteen minutes I had the picture installed like an actor in the dark with a light on it it was Godot as soon as the lecture was over people rushed up to the *detail* because of the power it was giving off for as long as I live I want to create spaces once I arrived in my space in Venice with Isy Brachot if I were you he says I'd put this photo here it's like a musical score I replied everything is in its place then in comes Günter Ueker and exclaims it's just like a score and I said to Isy now Isy you see difference between an artist and a gallery owner I can't ban arrangements I don't like but I do want people to know that the installation is part of the work it's the home of my whole conception and I can't bear people messing about with my work when I was awarded the Grand Prix National de Peinture the Pompidou Centre rushed to put three of my *details* on display and I was invited to come and look it was a total disaster they can't be hung like Impressionists or Magrittes I reject the spirit of the retrospective I don't want anyone touching this body standing in front of a *detail* should feel like standing in a doorway and each time you need to find just the right solution a space is a creation Helmut Friedel he put frames on them it was a complete betrayal there I was trying to preserve the purity of the canvas it makes me angry often I go in somewhere where my work is being shown I should be pleased but it's horrible a real torture to see one of my canvasses in a group exhibition hang them next to a Klein or a Fontana that's no problem they're from the same family one or two *details* properly hung in a collection is all right it can be fine but a whole set nobody else but me can install them properly if the space isn't right then you miss part of what I'm trying to say it's a sort of temple to time a temple to an existence the *details* are its columns you can be creative with the missing *details* as you can with missing columns there are different periods but the space forms a single body

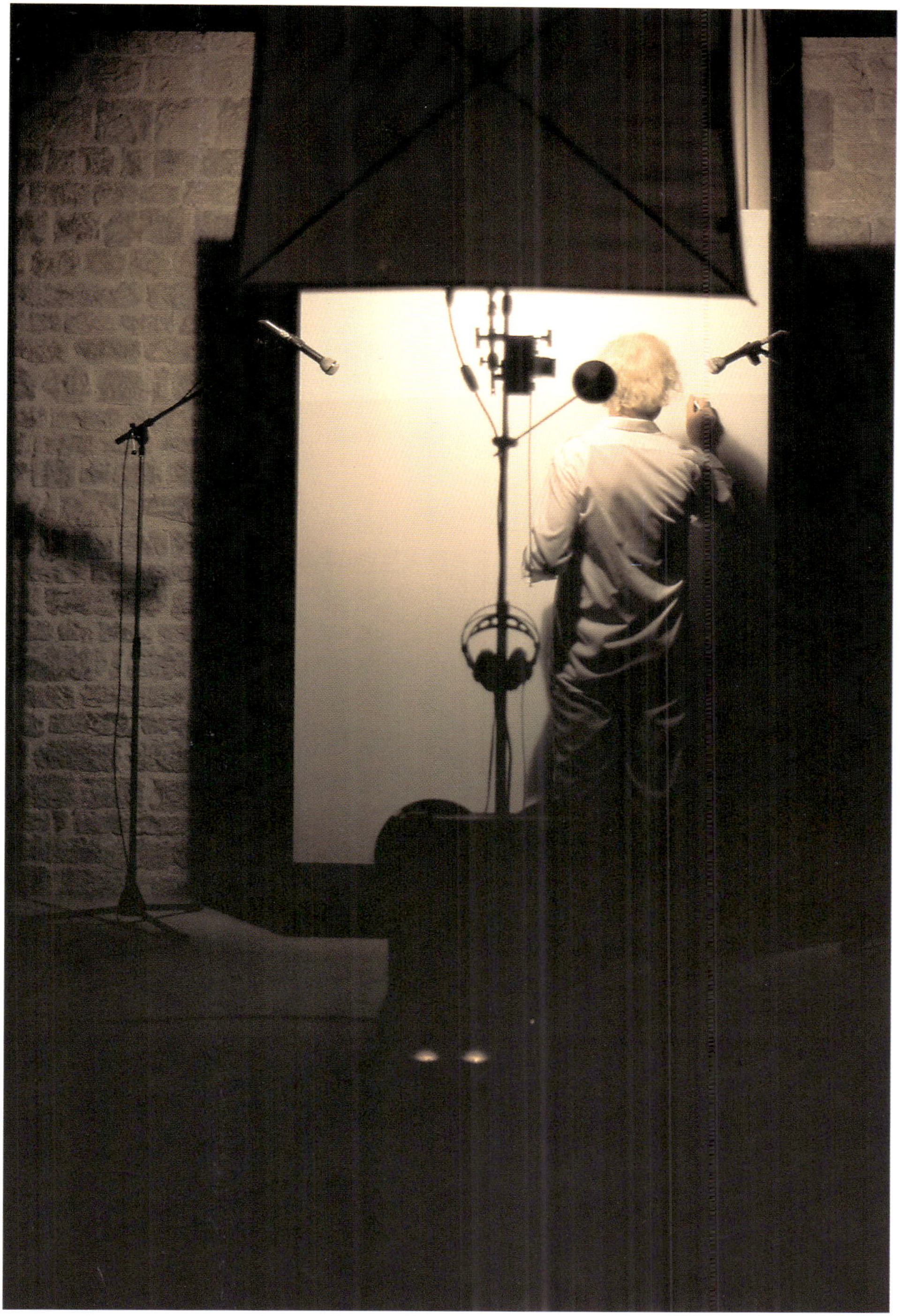

◄ 1

► 2

► 4

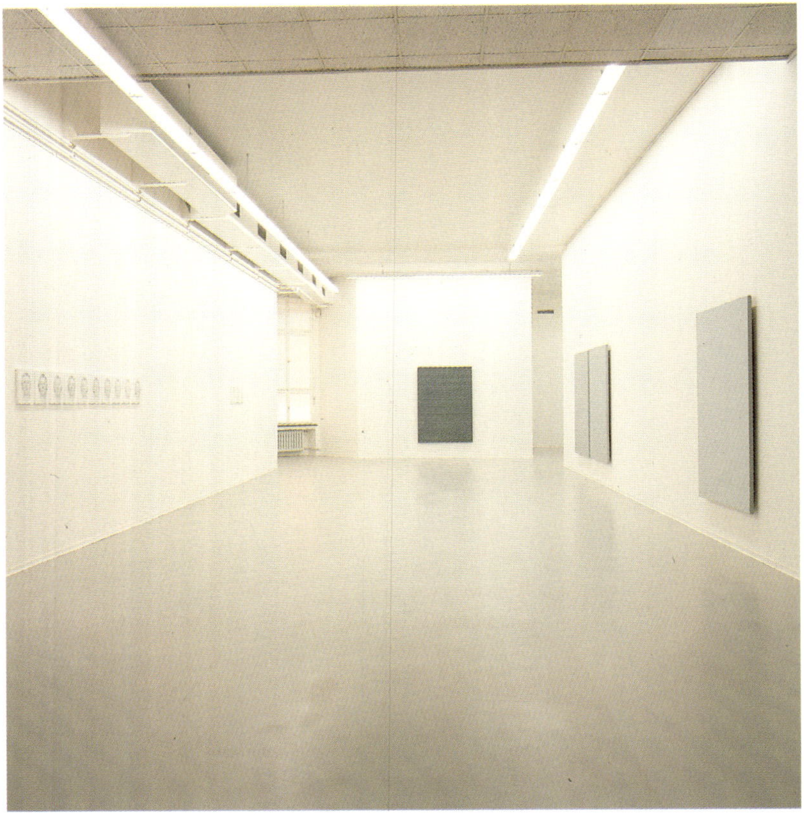

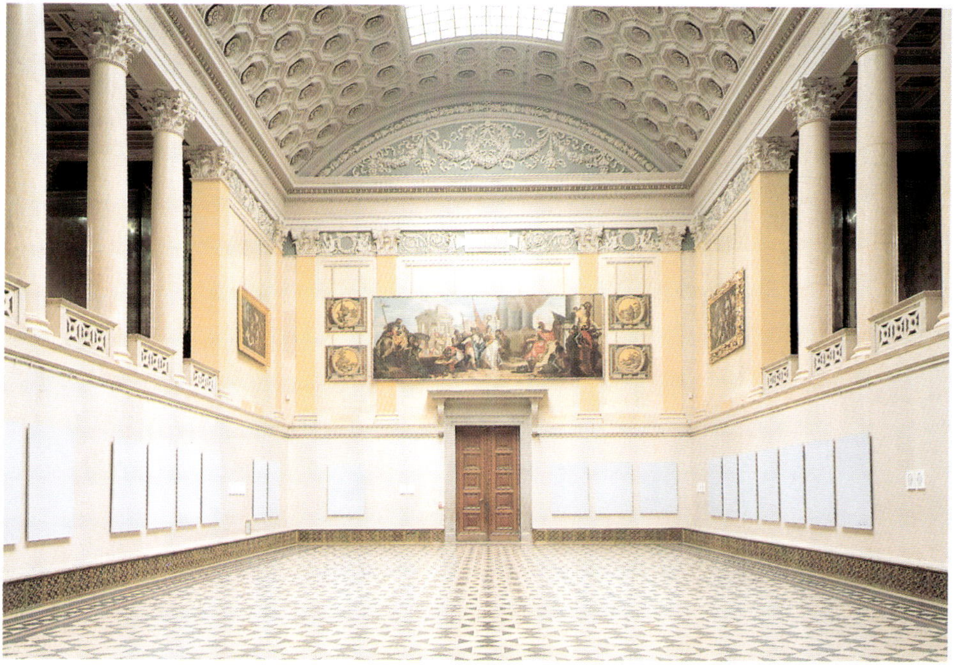

◄ 5

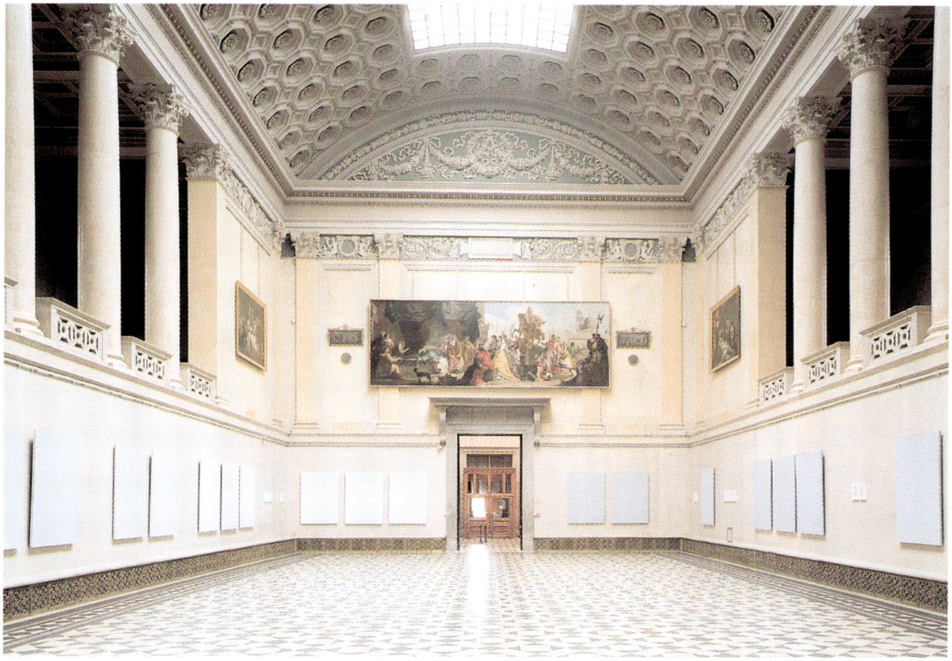

◄ 6

▶ 7

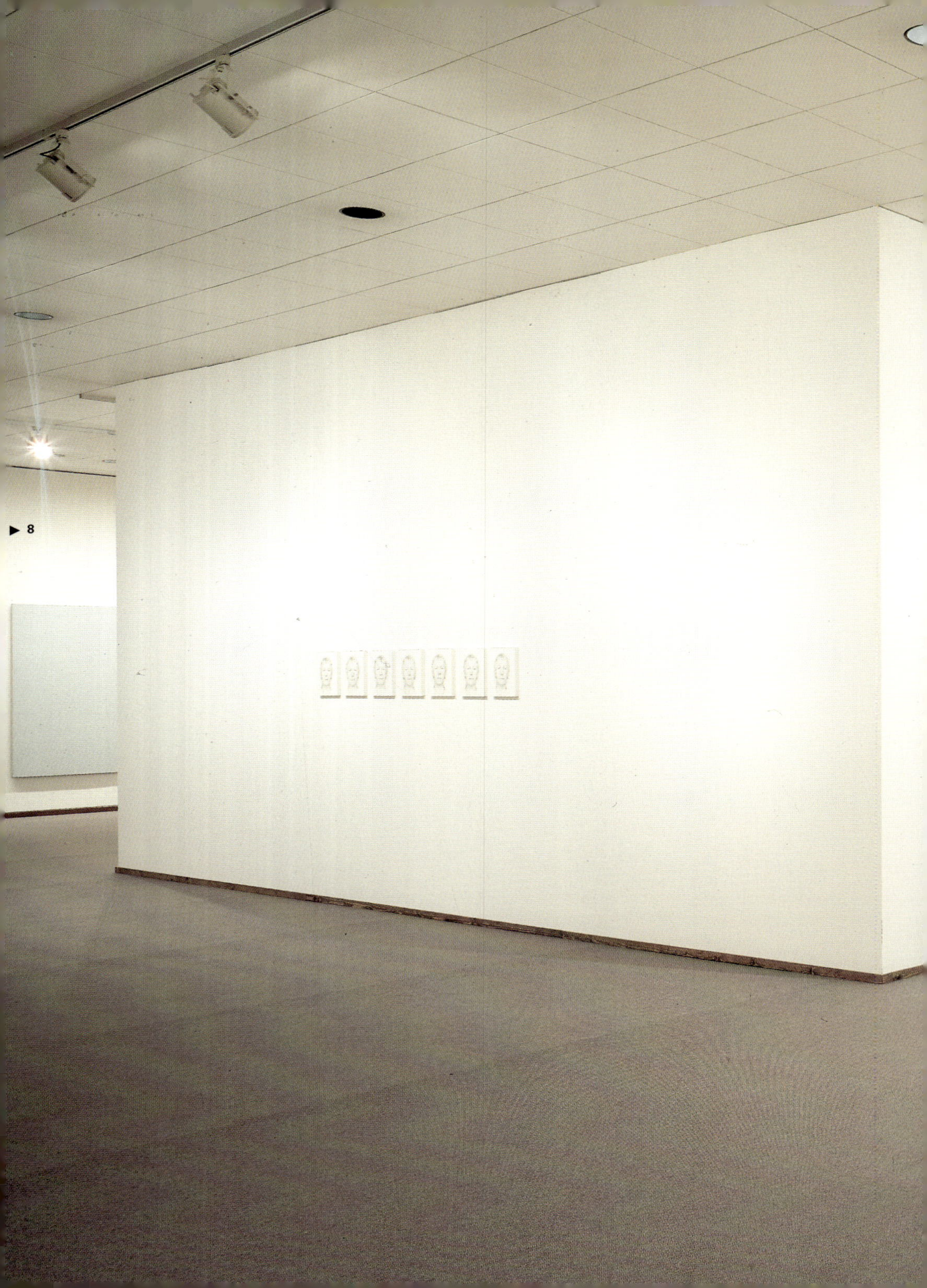

▶ 8

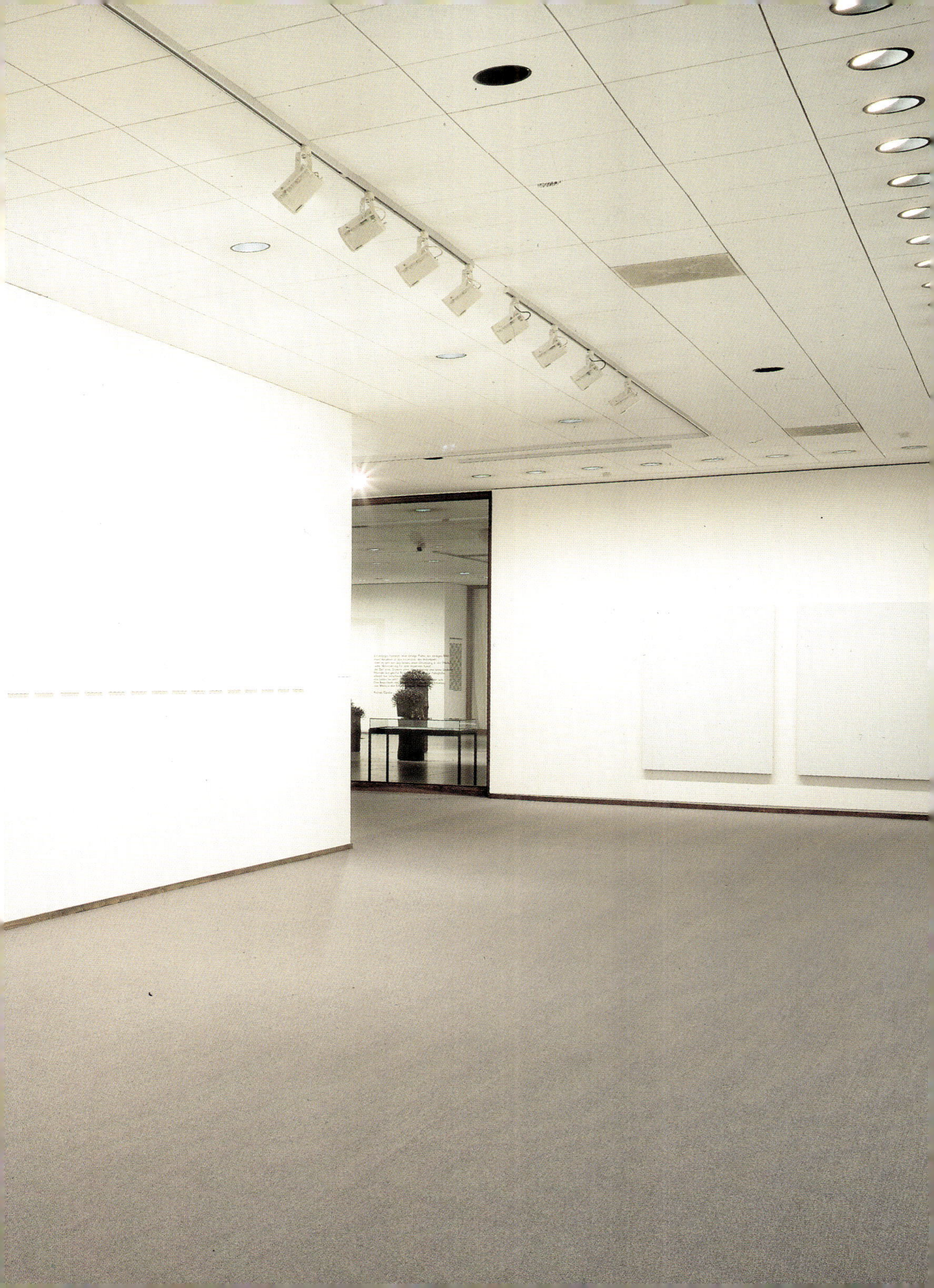

▶ 9

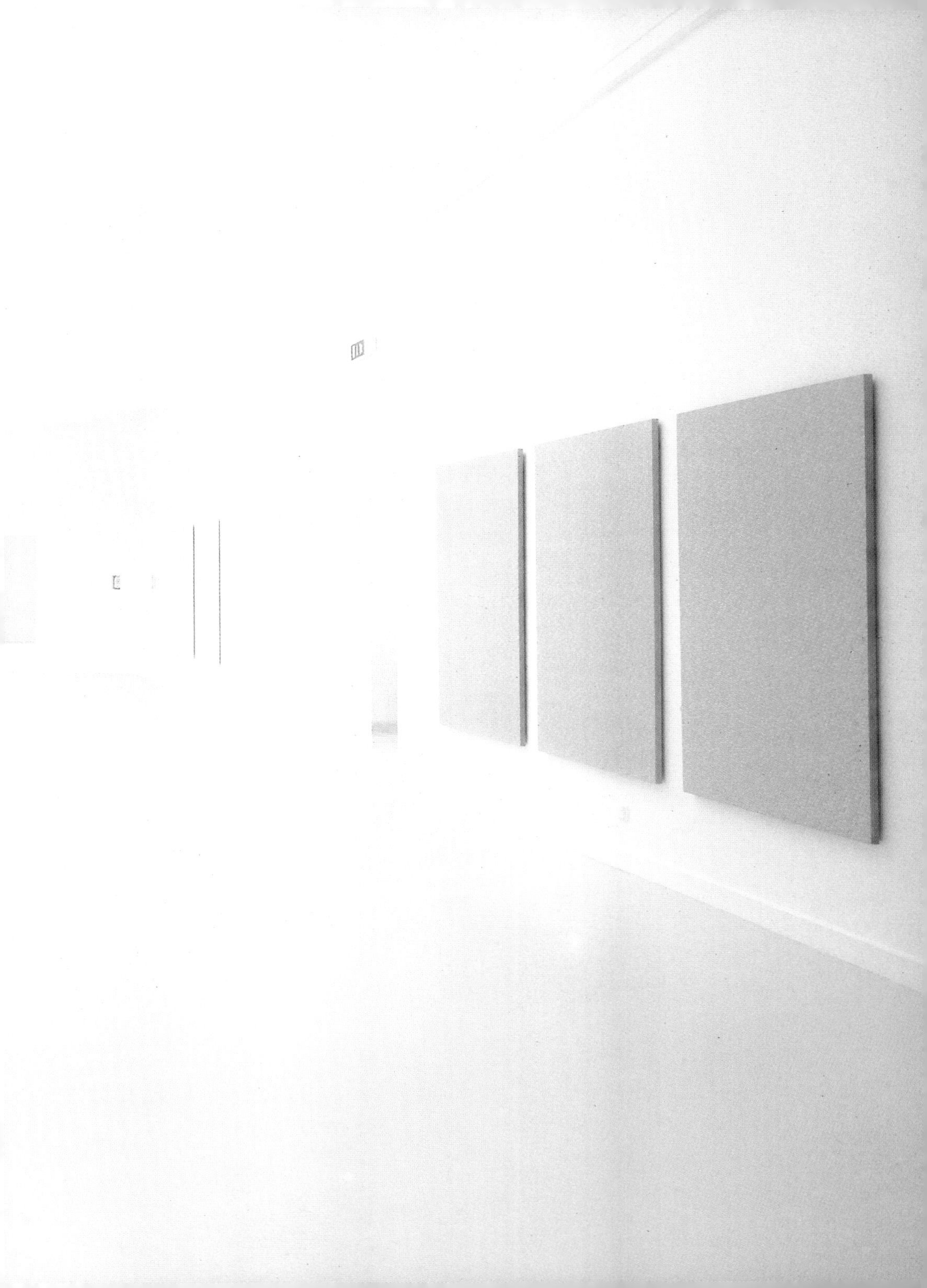

▶ 10

▶ 11

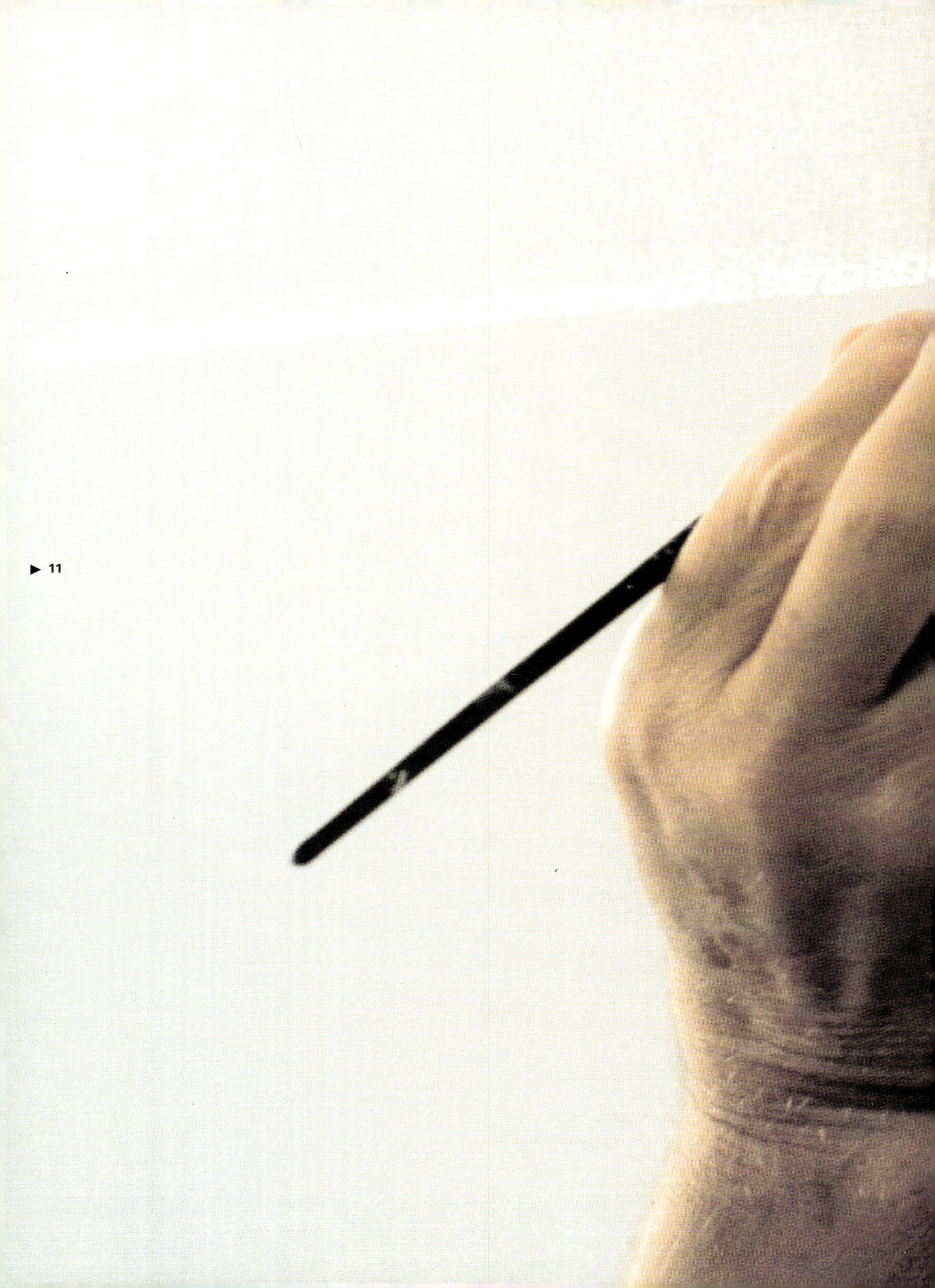

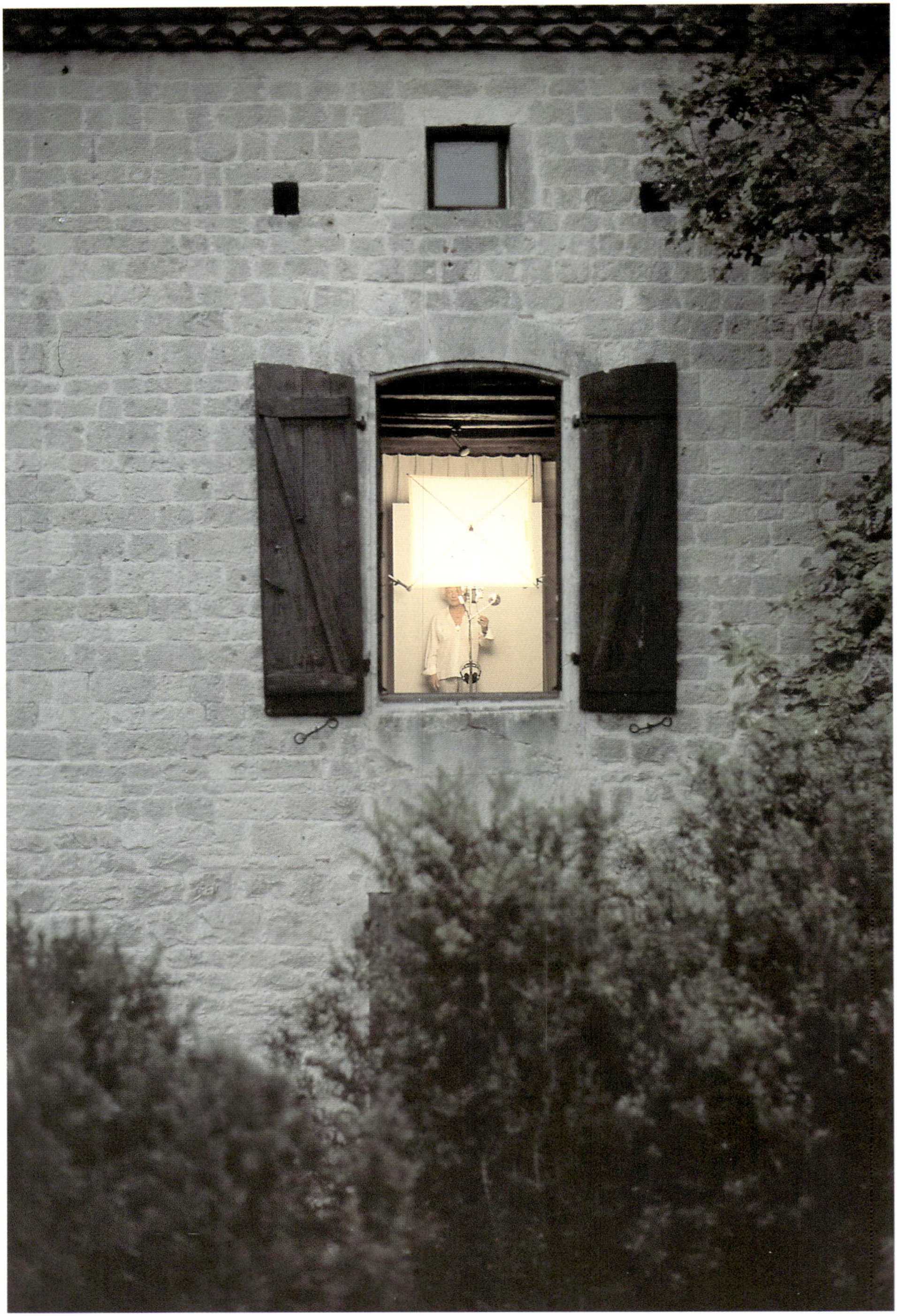

Photo Index

1: "The painter's verticality."

2: "OPALKA 1965/1-∞ *Détail* 1-35327", tempera on canvas."

" *Le* Détail-*painting is* part of a whole; *it is the Detail of a whole which is a single painting (the work* OPALKA 1965/1 - ∞). *There is an œuvre, there is a painting, the painting of an œuvre, just as there is an existence, a depth of time, the image of a life, a unity.*" [Roman Opalka]

3: "OPALKA 1965/1-∞ *Détail 5065513 - 5081904*", acrylic on canvas."

4: OPALKA Neues Museum Weserburg, Bremen, 1992.

"*An exhibition is an evocation of the essential: I must inhabit space like my home, I must dwell there and invite to a meditation on one thing: life.*" [Roman Opalka]

5/6: OPALKA Svepmuveszeti Muzeum, Budapest, 1995.

7: Musée de la Ville de Paris, Paris 1992.

8: Nationalgalerie, Berlin, 1994.

9: Biennale, Venice, 1995.

10: Biennale, Venice, 1995.

11: "Before the acrylic dries."

12: "With pictures of my face, I sculpt time."

About the Artist

Roman Opalka was born in France of Polish parents the 27 August 1931 in Hocquincourt, in the Somme. He studied in Lodz and Warsaw in Poland.
He has lived and worked in France since 1977.

Recent Personal Exhibitions

1990 Galerie Lallouz, Montreal, Canada.
Centre d'Art contemporain, Mont-de-Marsan.
École d'Art de Dunkerque, Dunkerque.
Galerie Le Chanjour, Nice.
Galerie Walter Storms, Munich.

1991 Galerie Isy Brachot, Brussels.
Primo Piano, Rome.
Mala Galerija, Moderna Galerija, Ljubljana.
Galeria Appendix, Warsaw.
Galerie du Triangle, Bordeaux.

1992 Galerie Christine et Isy Brachot, Paris.
Galerie Foksal, Warsaw.
Neues Museum Weserburg, Bremen.
Musée d'Art Moderne de la Ville, Paris.
Galerie Froment & Putman, Paris.
Städtische Galerie im Lenbachhaus, Munich.

1993 Museum moderner Kunst Stiftung Ludwig im Museum des 20. Jahrhunderts, Vienna.
Städtische Galerie, Göpingen.
Mönchehaus-Museum für moderne Kunst, Goslar.

1994 Stadt Fellbach.
Newe Nationalgalerie, Berlin.
Zacheta, Warsaw.

1995 Svepmuveszeti Muzeum, Budapest.
Biennale, Venice.

1996 Galerie I.S.M., Seoul.
Galerie Gain, Seoul.
Arsenal Galeria, Miejska Bwa, Poznan.
Starmach Galeria, Krakow.

Bibliography

Books

1991 Opalka Roman, “Rencontre par la séparation - Begegnung durch Trennung”, Munich, Verlag Walter Storms.

1992 Opalka Roman, “Opalka 1965/1 - ∞” Paris, Flammarion 4/la Hune

1994 Fréchuret Maurice, “La Machine à Peindre”, Marseille, Jaqueline Chambon.

1994-95 “Des Élèves à l’œuvre” (n°4), Fonds Régional d’Art Contemporain, Académie de Lille.

Films

1973 *Imiona Czasu*, director Franciszek Kuduk
Production Telewizia polska, Warsaw.

1986 *Détail - Roman Opalka*, director Christophe Loizillon,
Production Lazenec/la Sept, Paris. (First Prize, studio section, ex æquo)
1st Biennale Internationale du Film sur l'art, Paris, 1988.

1993 *Od jeden do nieskonczonosci/Roman Opalka*, director Franciszek Kuduk

Also available from Dis Voir

PLASTIC ARTS

François Dagognet
In Favour of Today's Art

Jean-Yves Bosseur
Sound and the Visual Arts

Thierry de Duve
Du Nom au Nous
La Déposition
Clement Greenberg between the lines
(including a previously unpublished debate with Clement Greenberg)

Rainer Rochlitz
(*with* Shusterman; Genette; Schaeffer; Bürger; Menke; Meschonnic; Jimenez; Chateau)
L'Esthétique des philosophes

Alain Charre, Marie-Paule MacDonald, Marc Perelman
Dan Graham

Christine Macel, Marc Perelman, Jacinto Lageira
Jean-Marc Bustamante

Gertrud Koch, Luc Lang, Jean-Philippe Antoine
Gerhard Richter

LITERATURE/FINE ART/CINEMA

Raúl Ruiz

Poetics of Cinema
The Book of Disappearances & The Book of Tractations
A la Poursuite de l'Ile au Trésor

Peter Greenaway

The Falls
Rosa
Fear of Drowning by Numbers
Papers - (Paintings, Collages and Drawings)
The Cook, the Thief, his Wife and her Lover
The Baby of Mâcon
The Pillow Book

Manoel de Oliveira

Les Cannibales
Lisbonne Culturelle

CINEMA

Paul Virilio, Carole Desbarats, Jacinto Lageira, Danièle Rivière

Atom Egoyan

Michael Nyman, Daniel Caux, Michel Field, Florence de Mèredieu, Philippe Pilard

Peter Greenaway

Christine Buci-Glucksmann, Fabrice Revault d'Allonnes

Raúl Ruiz

Yann Lardeau, Jacques Parsi, Philippe Tancelin

Manoel de Oliveira

CHOREOGRAPHY

Paul Virilio, René Thom, Laurence Louppe, Jean-Noël Laurenti, Valérie Preston-Dunlop

Traces of Dance - Drawings and Notations of Chor egraphers

(*with*: Bob Wilson; V. Nijinski; Merce Cunningham; Rudolf von Laban; Lucinda Childs; Trisha Brown; R.A. Feuillet; Ann Theresa de Keersmaeker; Mary Wigman; Dana Reitz; Philippe Decouflé; Dominique Bagouet; Daniel Larrieu; A. Lorin; J.Weaver; P. Rameau; M. Isaac; Hervé Robbe; Régine Chopinot; George Appaix; Jean-Marc Matos; K. Tomlinson; L.G. Pécour; R. Huilmand.)

ARCHITECTURE

Christian de Portzamparc

Genealogy of Forms

ÉDITIONS DIS VOIR: 3, RUE BEAUTREILLIS - F-75004 PARIS
PHONE (33) 01 48 87 07 09 - FAX (33) 01 48 87 07 14

ACHEVÉ D'IMPRIMER
EN OCTOBRE 1996
SUR LES PRESSES
DE
L'IMPRIMERIE F. PAILLART
À ABBEVILLE

DÉPÔT LÉGAL : 4e TRIMESTRE 1996
N°. IMP. 9895